OUT
OF THE
DARKNESS

OUT
OF THE
DARKNESS

A woman's journey through a childhood
and early life ravaged by alcoholism and
despair, into the light and arms of God.

Patricia Bennett LaPrise

~ ~ ~
Mason Marshall Press
Medford, Massachusetts

Published by Mason Marshall Press.

Copyright © 2020 by Patricia Bennett LaPrise
Cover copyright © 2020 by Mason Marshall Press.
All rights reserved.

ISBN-13: 9781632470386

Library of Congress Control Number: 2020931388

For information, please contact:
Mason Marshall Press
P.O. Box 324
Medford, MA 02155

PUBLISHED IN THE UNITED STATES OF AMERICA

Contents

Dedication vii

Author Note ix

Preface 1

One 5

Two 15

Three 28

Four.. 47

Five... 61

Six... 73

Seven 81

Eight... 91

Nine 103

Ten.. 121

Eleven 135

Twelve 149

My Life Now 175

Afterword... 178

The Caron Foundation 179

Thank You.. 180

Acknowledgements 181

Poems 183

Questions for Book Clubs and Discussion Groups........... 188

To my parents, who I loved more than life itself.

Author Note / Contact

Dear Reader,

To the best of my ability, I have tried to recreate events, locales, and conversations from my memories of them and through conversations with friends and relatives. In some instances, I have changed the name and/or identifying characteristics of individuals to protect the privacy of those living and the families of those deceased.

If you would like to contact me with a question or comment, you may do so via email to patricialaprise@masonmarshall.com or on Facebook at https://www.facebook.com/pblaprise

Patricia

Preface

In January 1991 I found myself traveling to a place in Wernersville, Pennsylvania called The Caron Foundation. I had no idea what to expect when I got there. What I did know was that this came highly recommended. It was a treatment center for adult children of alcoholics. I certainly fit that description. I was also an alcoholic who had been in recovery for five years. I went to a program to get help and went to meetings to learn about alcoholism, its affects, and how to not drink a day at a time.

I watched many people come into the program, saw them change as they worked the steps and put the principles to work in their lives, and witnessed them become different people. They were happy and free and I envied them. I wanted to feel that way, too. I didn't understand why it was not happening in my life. One day, a guy told me, "Some are sicker than others." Boy-oh-boy did that piss me off. I wanted to smack the crap out of him. In fact, most of the time I wanted to smack somebody for something they said or did.

The program had a lot of sayings to help people. While I loved some of them, like *One Day at A Time* and *Live and Let Live*, I despised others, like *Acceptance is the Key to My Recovery* and *Let Go Let God*. Everyone knew if I let go of anything, there would be claw marks. Besides, I had no idea what I needed to let go of. I was full of hurt, anger, resentment, and bitterness. I didn't know how to begin to let it go. It was recommended to me that I might try the Caron Foundation because I was raised in an alcoholic home.

I was desperate for help and so wanted the freedom I saw in others. I hated that I felt hurt and angry all the time and wanted more for my life. I wanted to be free from all the baggage I was carrying. Its weight had taken a toll on me. I didn't have many friends and the ones I did have were as messed up as me. We were like the blind leading the blind. Healthy people didn't want to hang out with me because I was toxic. One of my friends told me that people often referred to me as Angry Patty. I told her they were all jerks as I pounded my fist on my steering wheel, lamenting how mean it was for them to call me that. You can't see the apple that is on your own head and I certainly didn't see the one on mine. Why they would call me such a thing was a mystery to me. I honestly thought my anger was justified, and felt I had a right to be angry. That may have been true, but getting angry and staying angry are two different things. With me, it was like the anger had a life of its own.

There were a few times I felt free from the anger and self-hatred that plagued me, but they were fleeting. They were small, but very powerful glimpses into how freedom could feel. People in the program called these new feelings that newcomers get "pink clouds." I had my first pink cloud when I was about three months sober. It was my first taste of freedom and the happiness was so exciting, I penned this:

Pink Clouds

There are soft pink clouds beneath my feet
Such radiance within oh, how sweet
My warm tender heart is all aglow
These new feelings inside Lord, they frighten me so
For the once-stolen innocence of a young child's soul
Was restored by you father now I am whole
In excitement and wonder I go forth now free
For I accept who I am and I'm glad to be me

When I shared the poem with my sponsor, she said she loved it, but that "this too shall pass"—another saying in the program. When you're feeling bad and someone tells you, "this too shall pass," it brings you hope. But when you're feeling great and it's said, it really sucks. What the heck, I thought. I don't want this to pass.

Self-acceptance was a new concept to me. It felt good to think maybe I was worth something. It was nice feeling happy inside. But it did pass as she said it would, and I was back to feeling all the anger and hurt I'd been living with. It was a huge disappointment for me, although once I experienced this first taste of freedom, I wanted more. I wanted complete and lasting freedom. There was no going back to the person who didn't know the difference anymore. I tasted peace from all the turmoil for a brief day or two and now I hungered for more. I wanted complete freedom that was lasting. For me there was no going back. I would do everything I could to find the answers I needed.

In Chapter Five of the *Alcoholics Anonymous Big Book*, the chapter *How It Works* talks about the details of the program and what people need to do if they want recovery. In one place it states, "There are those, too, who suffer from grave emotional and mental disorders, but many of them do recover if they have the capacity to be honest."

After hearing this, I went into the bathroom and dropped to my knees crying. I remember begging God to help me be able to be completely honest. I knew I was a person who suffered from grave emotional problems. I was not sure it would be considered a disorder, but certainly there was something not right. I prayed I could be one of the ones who had the capacity to be honest. Clearly, I fit the description of a person with emotional problems. About the only emotions I felt were anger, frustration, and more anger. It was difficult enough to admit that to myself, but I knew I would have to admit it to someone else if I wanted to get help.

I spoke to some people in the program who told me about

The Caron Foundation. So here I was, heading out of New Hampshire to Pennsylvania, with hope, to a place where the light and love of God would shine. I would learn how—if only my mother had known about her frailties, if only she knew how fragile her ego was—perhaps she could have seen how her hurt, anger, and disappointment were destroying her adoring child.

This is a story about a child carrying the weight of her mother's hurt, anger, and bitterness through a world full of the unfriendliest of people stealing her innocence; through a world of darkness, void of her mother's love; a world where there was no safe place to turn; a world where her own self-hatred threatened to destroy her. I was that child, and this is my story.

One

I was born on Thursday evening March 25, 1954 around 6:00 pm. I weighed 4 ½ pounds. I had a two year old sister, and we lived with my dad's mother.

My parents lived with her since they married three years before. Well, not exactly from the day they got married. She and my dad decided to elope, so on Sunday afternoon, April 22, 1951, their friend John drove them to Salisbury, New Hampshire, and they got married. My mother just turned eighteen and my dad was turning seventeen the next day. They didn't dare tell anybody.

They returned to their homes, living life as they did before they married until one morning, my grandmother told my father to do something he didn't want to do. He yelled at her, "You can't tell me what to do! I'm married!"

After she figuratively picked herself up off the floor, she took him to get my mother to bring her to live with them. Mom and Dad lived with my grandmother and her five other children — his brothers Bobby, Charles, and Paul and his sisters Joan and Barbara.

My older sister Karen was born the following February 9, 1952, the day before my mother's nineteenth birthday. My mother had us kids at Boston City Hospital. Back in 1952 at that hospital, mothers were expected to breastfeed their babies.

They didn't give them a choice. My mother was very modest, and breastfeeding made her immensely uncomfortable. I guess by the time she left the hospital she was so nervous about the breastfeeding her milk dried up.

My sister was crying all the time because she was hungry and my mother had no idea what to do. She did not grow up with babies around and spent most of her youth at her grandmother's house because her mother had tuberculosis. She knew nothing at all about them, or about formula or sterilizing baby bottles. She was so frazzled that one afternoon she broke down crying and couldn't stop. My grandmother told her to get some rest; that she would take care of my sister for the rest of the day and not to worry.

Gram went to the store and bought bottles, Carnation milk, and Karo Syrup to make formula. She sterilized the bottles and filled them with the freshly made formula. When my mother woke up a few hours later my sister was content, sleeping peacefully. My grandmother knew all about babies.

My mother was raised in a home where she did not learn how to speak up for herself. She once told me that when Karen was born, she lived in a house with so many people, she didn't get to do much for her. She said that at

My mother and father at their wedding celebration

times, it seemed like Karen was not even her baby. She was only nineteen when Karen was born and never lived on her own, so I guess she just let everybody take over. My mother said she didn't even pick out my sister's name; my grandmother did. Mom said she made sure when I came along, she picked my name. She named me a combination of her and her mother's middle names — Patricia Eleanor.

Though we were still living with my grandmother when I was born, nobody seemed the least bit interested in me. They were still enthralled with Karen, leaving Mom with complete charge of my care. Because she had so much help with Karen, it was all new to her and childcare landed hard on her. She was overwhelmed with the responsibility. She needed children who were easy to care for and I was anything but that. Right from the get-go, I needed more attention from her than a newborn usually requires.

I was only 4 ½ pounds at birth, which scared the heck out of her. I was baptized in the hospital hours after my birth. I think that was standard procedure when a newborn was under five pounds at birth, but that scared my mother, too. Also, the nurse put too much Silver Nitrate in my eyes which was a very serious problem. This required me to have special treatments at the hospital three times a week. My mother told me I had to be seen Monday, Wednesday, and Friday at the clinic at Boston City Hospital for the next six or seven months. Right from day one, my mother felt burdened by my needs.

We lived in Roxbury, not too far from the hospital, but not walking distance. My mother said she had to take a bus down and back with my sister in tow and that it was a pain having to take the bus with an infant and a two-year-old. She hated it so much, her aunt Barbara, after whom she was named, offered to take me to my appointments. My great-aunt Barbara lived in Jamaica Plain, so she would travel by bus from Jamaica Plain to get me, take the bus to the hospital and back, then take another bus back home.

Aunt Barbara was nice. Throughout my childhood, she was the person who did special things for us kids, like buy us each a couple of dresses for the beginning of school. I can still remember the two dresses she bought me for first grade. I had my picture taken in one of them. My parents didn't have a lot of money, so it helped them a lot. Aunt Barbara also bought Karen and me our First Communion outfits. We were raised Catholic. The thing I liked best about getting new clothes was I got to go to Forrest Hills Factory Outlet, the store where my aunt worked, to pick them out. I loved going to the store and spending time with my mother and aunt. The dresses were nice, but it was nicer being with them.

My mother said I just stopped eating when I was about three weeks old. She had to bring me to the hospital and I was admitted for a couple of days for observation. When my mother returned to pick me up, she said the doctor told her he could not find anything wrong with me. He told her I just needed more attention; that she should hold me when she fed me, not prop my bottle. She came to deeply resent me. I always felt like she hated me. I think that was the start of me being her scapegoat. It seemed like she believed I did it on purpose to annoy her. She told me many times — and didn't say it in a nice way — that I should have been born an only child because I needed too much attention. Lucky for me we lived with my grandmother.

Her friend Ida would attend to me at night, giving my mother a break and me the much-needed attention. Apparently, she would stop by my grandmother's after work and take over my care for the evening. Many times growing up, my mother told me that story along with the one of how easy Linda was; how she would sleep twelve hours straight. My mother said she used to have to wake her up. Thank God for my grandmother's friend helping my mother. I loved Ida and can still remember everything about her. She and my grandmother were lifelong friends.

We lived with my grandmother until I was about six months old. Then my parents moved into their first apartment alone with Karen and me. By that time, my mother was pregnant with my sister Linda, who would be followed by Rick, Stephen, and Paula. Children came quickly back then with no real reliable birth control.

My mother loved having her own apartment with my dad and things were going pretty well for them living alone. She told me she would play ghost with me and Karen all the time; that we would run around and laugh. She loved playing with us and making us laugh. She said one time she was not paying attention and fell down the stairs because she didn't have holes in the sheet to see. I guess she didn't get hurt but said she was more careful after that. She said that was the happiest she ever was. Then my dad turned twenty-one years old and was off and running.

He would go to the bars pretty much every night and some nights would not come home. She knew he was running around on her. My mother was naive back then, having grown up sheltered for the most part. She thought if the women in the bar knew he was married they would not go out with him. So, she would wheel Linda and me in the carriage and Karen next to it holding the handle down to the bar early in the evening some nights so the women could see us. Of course, that didn't change a thing. I have no idea how many times she did that, and though Linda and I were much too young to have any clue what we were doing, I wonder what Karen might have thought about it since she was two years older.

My family had issues. All families do. For good or ill, we are all impacted by our family. My mother and father were not different in the sense they both had issues. Each brought baggage from their own childhoods into their marriage.

My dad was an alcoholic and womanizer. I can't say what caused these behaviors, but here are some contributing factors I know about. My dad once told my mother he had been grabbed at the Boy's Club when he was around thirteen. He said some guy tried to get fresh with him but that he got away. I suspected he did not get away; that he carried so much shame, it contributed to both his drinking and womanizing. I thought he might be trying to prove to himself that he was a man. Of course, this is just speculation on my part. I have no way of knowing for sure.

He was also driven by a lot of fear. He had six kids by the time he was twenty-six years old. He told my mother once when we were all grown that he was always so afraid when we were little. That he was scared to death he would not be able to support us, get us the things we needed like food, shelter, and clothing.

Of course, in those days, men didn't tell people they were afraid of anything. Also, child molestation was just not talked about. If that *was* an issue, he never would have been able to tell anyone about it. He would have had to suffer in silence. I can understand how that might have driven him to the arms of other women, as well as deep into the bottle.

As I said, they each brought baggage into their marriage. My mother was always moving between her parents' and her maternal grandparents' houses. Her mother had tuberculous and was in and out of sanitariums.

My mother developed rheumatic fever when she was ten. Her mother was home from the sanitarium and cared for her for a year until she made a full recovery. Not long after my mother was well, her mother passed away. My mother was just eleven years old. As she grew up, Mom said she always felt it was her fault her mother died; that the stress of caring for her for the year she was sick was what killed her mother. It wasn't until my mother was in her mid-forties that her father told her how her mother really died. Apparently, she went into the hospital for surgery that was supposed to help cure her TB and she got pneumonia. They didn't have antibiotics back then, so she died from the pneumonia.

How my mother learned of her mom's death was quite traumatic. She went shopping for a new skirt and sweater with her maternal grandmother at one of the big department stores in downtown Boston. When they arrived home, one of the neighborhood boys saw my mother walking up the street with her grandmother. He yelled to her, "So I hear your mother died. How do you like that, Barbara?" My mother was crushed. She told me her father didn't have much sympathy for her. She said he came across the street after her mother had been brought home to be waked, took her and her younger sister by the hand into the living room where her mother lay, and told them to take a look at the most beautiful woman in the world because they were never going to see her again. He then took them back across the street to their maternal grandmother's house. I don't believe my mother was allowed to go to the funeral.

After her mother died, my mother went to live with her maternal grandmother, who she adored. She was just thirteen when her grandmother died and it devastated her. She moved from one aunt to another for the reminder of her teen years and never knew from day to day where she would be living. The only time she saw her father was when he would drop by to give her money to get something she needed.

My mother had a sister and a brother. They lived with her dad and her other grandmother across the street. Her grandparents on both sides were neighbors all her life. Her mother and father grew up together on Lee Street in Jamaica Plain. Their parents each moved to Lee Street from other countries. Her maternal grandparents came from Scotland. Her grandfather came to the US from Glasgow when he was fourteen or fifteen. He sent for my great grandmother when she turned eighteen. She was from Edinburgh. My mother's paternal grandparents came here from Dublin, Ireland.

The deaths of her mother and grandmother caused my mother to have abandonment issues. Along with the fact her father was an alcoholic, she was ripe to be the perfect codependent wife.

In those days, little was known about codependence. Alcoholics Anonymous had only been in existence since 1935 — barely twenty years old. Al-Anon, created in 1951, was still in its infancy. Few people even knew about it. I did have an aunt who knew about it and told my mother, but my mother never went to it.

* * *

Every society has what are considered social norms — the unwritten rules which govern our behavior. Providing order and predictability within society, they are expectations for us and vary from culture to culture. When greeting people in our Western culture, we often shake hands. In Eastern cultures, it is customary to bow. These are both taught at an early age. There are also societal norms that are often unspoken. Nobody tells you, but somehow we learn things like, don't stand in someone's personal space, stand on the right side of the escalator leaving a space on the left for people to walk by, and let people out of an elevator before you enter.

Families are like small societies and they have certain norms as well. They vary from family to family according to family values. Some are traditional, in which we are taught

- Always say please and thank you
- Wash your hands before coming to the table
- Say "excuse me" if you burp or fart

and those sorts of things.

Others are unspoken. No one tells you, but you learn what they are through observation. Our family was no different than others in this regard. We had a lot of the usual spoken rules. In addition, there were things like:

- Crying is not allowed
- Never show fear because it is a sign of weakness
- Wanting or needing something is selfish
- Don't talk about what happened last night
- Always pretend everything is alright
- If you don't stop crying I'll give you something to cry about.

We had others as well. Some of the rules were arbitrary. Depending upon who you were, some applied to you while others didn't. Also, they could change depending on the situation. For example, I was the one expected to be tough. I was the fighter in the family. I could be counted on to help protect the younger kids. That said, if one of my siblings did end up in a fight, they had better not get caught backing down or they would face my mother's wrath. Also, although you were expected to fight if someone was picking on you, you best not be caught starting a fight. Either of those offenses would get you an ass whooping you would never forget.

I witnessed both firsthand. One day, when I was headed home, I saw my mother with a group of people watching two kids. I realized one of them was my five-year-old brother. Someone was picking a fight with him. You could tell he didn't want to fight because he looked afraid and was crying. My mother was yelling that he better not be a coward. That he needed to stand up for himself; that if he didn't fight, she would give him a beating. He did fight of course. I felt so sad for my brother. I could not understand my mother being able to watch her children fight.

Another house rule was that we could not start a fight. I almost got myself spanked when my mother saw me chasing a girl who went over a fence and up a tree with me on her heels. My mother was screaming at me to get in the house when a neighbor told her the girl had been picking on me all day. My mother stopped yelling at me and left me alone. I could never understand my mother's thinking.

Most important of all was the two-part rule of all rules, the Cardinal Rule: Never disagree with my mother no matter what, and never take anyone else's side against her. Basically, you were either for her or against her. There was no middle ground. This rule applied to everyone, including my father, and was not to be broken. If she was mad at someone, you better be mad at them too. It didn't matter if it was your brother, sister, or even father. She was always mad at him and me, and because she was always mad at me, so was my older sister and, as the years went by, the other siblings as well. I felt so alone in a house of eight people.

When I was two years old, a few days after my brother was born, my mother told my father to leave. She told me I ran into the kitchen, got a brown paper bag, and started throwing my diapers and clothes in it saying, "I go daddy." She told me years later she hated me from that minute on. My two-year-old rejection hurt her more than her fragile ego could take.

Apparently, the night she went into labor he came home drunk, went to bed, and was asleep when her water broke. When she woke him to take her to the hospital, he started screaming at her. He screamed all the way to the hospital where he pulled up in front of the Emergency entrance, told her to get out, and sped away. She did not see his face again until she returned home four days later. She told him to leave.

Of course, I didn't know why she kicked him out. I didn't

know how broken her heart was. I only knew my dad was always nice to me. He made me feel special. He never yelled at me like my mother did. I only knew I loved him and was not afraid of him at that point.

After my dad left, my mother knew she could not afford the apartment we lived in, so she moved us to a low-income place, the Bromley Heath Housing Project. I can still remember the address: 940 Parker Street, Jamaica Plain, Mass 02130.

My dad ended up moving back in with us a few weeks after we moved there.

The Bromley-Heath housing project I lived in.

Two

Early Years

We moved into Bromley Heath in 1956. It was a time of racial unrest in our country and it was a scary place to live when I was little. We lived on the third floor of a seven-story building.

The project had both blacks and whites in disproportionate numbers. Each floor had four units, one occupied by a black family and three by white families. It was not a fair system, but as a small child, I didn't know that. All I knew was that we all lived and played together. I didn't know anything about racism. I was a child living in a place with other children, and though they had different color skin, they were like me as far as I was concerned. They were my friends. I suppose the black children probably felt the same, but the adults, white and black, felt different.

As a child, I knew the adults around us were mad at each other. The black adults mostly seemed to be mad at the whites, though I didn't know why. I do now, of course. Being treated unfairly caused them to resent whites. Having been treated unfairly within my family created a lot of resentment in me, so I understand now how being treated unfairly caused them to resent us white people. But as a child, I didn't understand why they were mad at us. We all lived together in the same circumstances.

As a small child, it was difficult to witness the anger and violence that resulted from it. It was scary to walk out my door each day and have to fight on the way to school. It was not the white boys from our neighborhood fighting with me. It was not the black girls either. I was friends with most of them. It was the young black boys. I hated fighting and did not understand why they wanted to beat me up just because I was white. They had no other reason to fight with me.

It was also scary at night listening to the gangs of black men drinking and smashing beer bottles on the pavement under my bedroom window. Those nights I could not sleep until I knew my dad was home. My fear increased when I learned a group of black teens pulled up in front of our building at dinner time one night and used a wine bottle to knock our neighbors' teeth out. He was the smallest guy in our building. I didn't witness it, but saw him the next day. He wouldn't hurt a flea. He was just washing his car.

I was terrified when the lady who lived in the unit below us was looking for my mother. She had a meat fork concealed under her coat. She was telling people she was going to kill my mother. Someone called the police and she was arrested. I was always afraid of her after that. It also scared me that my dad, a good fighter, could get his leg cut open by a group of black teens while he was changing his tire. He had a lot of stiches and carried a scar about eight inches long the rest of his life.

I didn't hate black people back then, and still don't, but I would be lying if I said I have never been afraid of some of them. Witnessing violence daily will do that. To this day, I fear *any* group of people who are angry at another group. I fear the mob mentality and the possibility it might get out of control. My mother taught us to respect all people. When I was a child, we had a black babysitter. He was fifteen and he was our favorite babysitter. We all loved him because he was much nicer than our white boy babysitter.

* * *

The violence outside my house was not the only violence I witnessed. There was an extreme amount of domestic abuse, as well as mental abuse to contend with in my home. I was as afraid to be in the house as I was to be out of it, though I never voiced it to anyone. I played the tough-as-nails girl, but perhaps it was not an act. I'm not sure so many years later. Perhaps I became that person to hide the fear even from myself. Whatever the reason, I became a walled off broken little bird.

My dad became a monster at times. When he came home from the bar at night, he would be drunk and would fight with my mother. I didn't see it when I was young, but I heard it all — my father yelling and cursing, the crying and screaming from my mother, and glass smashing on the floor.

I think my dad was hungry after drinking because when he came home, he would look in the fridge. Usually, there was not much food in there, just condiments like catsup, mustard, mayo and maybe some old, old leftovers. I think he would get mad because he wanted something to eat. Or perhaps he felt guilty seeing the empty refrigerator. Who knows? Looking in the fridge would sometimes send him into a rage. If he found something that was spoiled, he would lose it and scream at my

Age 3

mother about not cleaning the refrigerator. Then he would proceed to empty it by throwing its contents onto the kitchen floor. Back in those days everything came in glass containers. They would smash into pieces when they hit the floor. I can still remember the sound of the glass shattering. I would lie in bed covering my ears crying, hating what was happening and wanting it to stop. I didn't want to be there, and more than a few times, I wished I was dead because it hurt too much and I felt helpless.

My father didn't just smash stuff, he would hit my mother too. I knew because I could hear her scream. Some nights when the noise stopped, I would sneak out to make sure my mother was ok. I was afraid and would walk as quiet as I could on my tip toes to the kitchen. I would breathe a sigh of relief when I saw her. I guess I was afraid he might kill her by mistake. One night, when I got to the kitchen, I saw my mother sitting on the floor crying. She was soaked. My dad had dumped the pan with the boiled dinner she saved for him onto the floor, then pushed her. She slid across the greasy floor and fell. I remember thinking she looked so small and helpless sitting there crying. It was heartbreaking to see her like that and I hated my father for doing that to my mom.

Sometimes she would let me help clean up the kitchen. Other times, she would yell at me to get back to bed. I never knew what to expect so it was scary, but I felt compelled to check on her even if it meant getting yelled at. I guess I needed to be sure she was okay before I could go back to sleep.

There were times she would come into our room when she was hurt. My sisters and I shared a double bed and she would crawl in with us. One night, during the winter I was in the first grade, when she came in she said, "He banged my head." She was crying, saying over and over, "My head hurts." She had a huge bump, which scared me. I wanted to bawl my eyes out but didn't. I had to be strong. I kept rubbing her head and telling her it was going to be okay until I fell asleep. I felt so alone all the time, like the weight of the world was on my shoulders.

I often wondered why the fighting never woke my sisters, especially my older sister, as it did me. I knew she would know what to do because she always seemed to know what to do. When we were older, she told me she didn't wake up most of the time because the fights had become so routine, she could sleep through them. I envied that. I could never sleep through them. I would wake up nights even when there was no fighting. Even today if I go to bed before midnight, I find myself waking around 1:00 am.

Being so young, it was hard for me to grasp that it was my father yelling because he was always so nice and at that time, never yelled around us kids. But I knew it was him. I recognized his voice. It was my dad but somehow, he turned into a monster I was afraid of. He was the person who would come home in the wee hours of the morning drunk and turn my world upside down.

* * *

How I Feared the Night

When I was young and innocent, oh how I feared the night
For darkness brought the devil home with all his fiery fright
At one AM the bars would close and soon he would appear
His breath would reek of whisky, sometimes rum or beer
Like Dracula in late night shows he was looking just for blood
The piercing screams would reach my room
The tears my eyes would flood
The pain and anguish of my soul was more than I could bear
The man who beat my mother up just didn't seem to care
This wasn't any stranger, I knew his voice real well
By day he was my father, by night a spawn from hell
His weapons were his fists and words, his home a place to fight
And I became a broken child who could not sleep at night
Oh God, I pray my father, never ever knows
The pain he caused his daughter with his late-night horror shows

* * *

My dad was not the only one to cause violence in our home. There were times my mother would completely lose control, like she lost her mind. Her behavior would be as crazy as my dad's when he was cleaning out our refrigerator breaking stuff, but when she lost it, she would hit someone. Usually, but not always, it was me.

There was a time when I was around ten and my dad came in drunk around five o'clock at night. He didn't say anything;

just went to bed. My mother was so mad at him she grabbed the wooden clothes rack and started beating him with it. Their bedroom had big double doors that opened into the living room. The doors were open and all us kids could see her breaking the rack on him as he lay defenseless in the bed. My older sister and I ran into the bedroom and stood next to the bed watching her hit him. I was crying, begging her to stop. Neither of us knew what to do. He was mostly covered up with a sheet and blanket, but I could see his chest because it was exposed. It was beat red with welts all over it where the rack was hitting. I could hear the little kids in the living room crying and screaming. My dad was saying over and over, "Barbara stop. Stop you're going to kill me." I thought she really was going to kill him because we could not make her stop. We had to call the police. I think my older sister was the one who called.

When the police came, they told my dad that he had to go with them for his own protection. He went in one police car. The rest of us went in another police car. They took us to my grandfather's house; my mother's father. I don't remember what they did with my mother, but I think she was with us.

Many years later my sister, Linda, asked me if I remembered that night. Of course, I did. How could I ever forget it! I had nightmares about it. I could not believe my mother did that. It gave me a whole new fear of my mother. I knew I better not make her mad at me anymore. Of course, that was impossible. She was always mad at me.

I didn't understand why my folks went kind of crazy at times, but I knew they were not bad people. I loved them both. I didn't understand until I got into recovery that my parents were both very hurt, broken people. One of the things I learned in recovery is that hurt people "hurt people."

As I said earlier, a few weeks after we moved into the project, my dad moved back in with us. As the program would say he was "back in the big bed."

Remember that cardinal rule we had—Never take anyone's side but my mother's in an argument. I learned that rule by the age of five. My mother and I had a volatile relationship right from the start. She was always telling me I was just like my father. Although, I knew there were good things about him, I knew she meant it in a bad way. She would tell me I was a little bitch. She said I was bold. I was too young to know what bold meant, but I knew it was a bad thing to be if she called me it. I was not a crier but when she said mean stuff to me, I would cry my eyes out. I would rather have a beating than her mean words. She knew it, too, which is why she did it. She wanted to make me hurt and somehow I knew it, which only made me feel worse. It sucked to think she wanted to hurt me; to make me cry. Sometimes I would tell her I hated her, then run into another room.

Whenever my dad heard her calling me names, he would tell her to stop. He didn't like it one bit. Sometimes they would get into a fight over me. He would tell her she should try being nice to me.

My mother told me that one day, when my dad was walking home from work, he heard her screaming at me as he was walking under the bridge. She told me he was upset when he came through the door because she was calling me names. She said she told him I "honey and deared" her all day and that I was a little bitch and he better not say one word to her about her yelling at me anymore. I guess my father never said another word because he knew he would never win that fight. His sticking up for me really pissed her off and there would be a price for it, a price extracted from me. She couldn't hurt him, but she could hurt me, so she indirectly paid him back for trying to protect me by hurting me.

I hated it when they would fight over me because I knew it was only going to make things worse. I can't tell you how I knew it, but I did. There was a look she would give me when my dad was not looking; a smile that would say, "You're in trouble now." That kind of thing. It was subtle, but I could feel it. I could sense the rage beneath her smile.

I loved my father fiercely, except for the nighttime monster, but he was making my life harder with my mother by defending me. The things he did at night caused such bitterness inside her that she resented my relationship with him.

Around the age of five, I made a decision which would define and damage my relationship with my father; one that would put me at odds with him.

Something happened between me and my mother. I don't remember what, but I was angry, so I told her I was running away. Since I didn't have a plan, I had to come up with one. I decided to hide in the front of the building where my mother could not see me if she looked out the window. Our windows were on the other side of the building. I wanted my mother to believe I ran away so she would think I was gone forever. I was hoping she would feel bad that I was gone. I stood on my tip toes with my back against the brick building, pressing as hard as I could, thinking I was hiding. I thought the ledge from the roof would help hide me from view if my mother looked out the hall window on that side of the building. The roof was seven stories above me. I thought she would never find me there, but secretly hoped she would try. I stayed out there for a long time, from after school until long after dark. Finally, I got too afraid to stay outside any longer. I went into the house feeling sad she didn't care enough about me to come find me, but also dreading her anger. When I walked in, I could tell she was mad at me. In her mean voice she said, "Your father wants to talk to you. He is in the bedroom." I was surprised he was home. He never came home that early. I was also afraid because I had never been in trouble with my dad before and thought he might spank me.

I was shaking like a leaf as I walked down the hall to his bedroom. He was sitting on the corner of his bed. The room was dark, but I could see him because the bathroom light was on. As I approached, he told me my mother said I ran away. He picked me up, put me on his lap, hugged me, and told me he loved me. Then he said he didn't want me to run away again. He told me if I had a problem, I should tell him about it so he could try to fix it for me; that from now on, when I was upset with my mother, he wanted me to come talk to him. He made me promise to never run away again. Then he put me on the floor and I walked out of the bedroom. As I reached the doorway, I looked back and saw him still sitting on the corner of the bed. He looked so sad it made me want to cry. I remember feeling bad because at that moment I knew that no matter how much he wanted to help me, he could not. At that age, I realized he was unable to even help himself. I walked away knowing I would never go to him for help and I never did. That was the night I rejected the one person in my house who I knew for sure loved me. It is one of the most painful memories I have to this day.

When I was little, I loved my mother as much as I loved my father. I thought she was beautiful, but I did not know how to get her to love me. It seemed no matter what happened, somehow, it was my fault. When I would get in arguments with my sisters, and she would hear me yelling, she would get mad at me. I would try to explain what I was yelling about, but she would not listen and I would be punished in some way. Usually, it was nothing serious. I hated knowing she was mad at me again, though it seemed like she always was. Still, I loved her and liked spending time alone with her. We seemed to get along okay when Karen was not around.

In first grade, completely by accident, I found a way to spend time with her. One day, just before lunch, I told my teacher I had to go to the bathroom. She told me no, it was quarter of twelve and only fifteen minutes until lunch and I could wait. But I could not hold it and ended up wetting my pants. My mother had to come to school and bring me home. When we got home, she told me to go change. When I came back into to the living room, I saw she set up my lunch on the coffee table. She told me I could have lunch and watch TV with her.

I wet my pants a lot in first grade and it was always just before lunch. She would pick me up and never hollered at me or anything. She would just set my lunch on the coffee table and after I changed, I would eat and watch television with her.

I loved those days with her.

When I was an adult, we talked about how I wet my pants in first grade. I asked her if she knew why. She said she talked to my teacher who said I was just immature but that it would get better. I told my mother I thought it happened so I could go home and spend time with her. She laughed and said, "It never occurred to me that it was on purpose because it would have been so out of the ordinary for you to deliberately do something like that." Looking back, though, she said it made sense. I can't say for sure what I was thinking way back then, but I do remember being happy each time I was sent home at lunch. It is a great memory I have of spending time with my mother.

* * *

Age 8

I believed I was the bad one in the family. I would go to school crying most days because my mom and I would fight before school. I would feel so bad as I walked out the door, knowing she was mad at me. One of us was usually yelling at the other and lots of times it was me doing the screaming.

Often, I didn't want to get up in the morning. I was beyond tired, but what does a six-year-old know? Only that she is tired. My six-year-old little brain couldn't comprehend what was happening to me; why I woke up so often angry. All I knew was I was tired and wanted to sleep.

When I was older, I came to realize all my mother wanted was to wake us up for school and have us all get up without all the yelling. She wanted compliant kids in the morning but I was not that kid. I was mad the mornings she was making cream of wheat instead of oatmeal for breakfast because the oatmeal filled my belly. She didn't know how to cook cream of wheat right and it was always so thin you could drink it. I hated soup for the same reason. I didn't want to drink my food; I wanted something that filled me up. I was hungry a lot. We all were. Those mornings might have been hard, but you could look forward to snack time at school.

My mother did always try to pack us a decent lunch. By decent I mean a sandwich, usually peanut butter and jelly or peanut butter and marshmallow, cupcakes or cake, and chips. On cream of wheat days, I could usually look forward to lunch filling my belly. But then there were days when I would find a cheese sandwich with mustard and nothing else. I could never choke it down no matter how hungry I was. It always found the trash bucket. And when cream of wheat and cheese sandwich days coincided, I spent the day so hungry I could not concentrate at school. My stomach would feel sick from smelling all the lunches in the coat closet.

I still remember how the school building smelled in the morning – too many lunch smells. Oranges, tuna fish, pickles, sandwich meats and more all mixed together in the coat closets. It was so pungent I hated the smell of school early mornings. Overall, though, I did like school itself.

I always knew what was expected of me, so I never got into trouble. I always tried my hardest and always got an A+ for effort. My third-grade teacher Mrs. Young was my all-time favorite. I loved her. Every Monday, she put a poem on the side blackboard. The whole class had to read it aloud every day and everyone was expected to know it on Friday. They were not long poems and I loved them because they usually meant something to me. Learning them made me feel like I could do something important well. Other things, like math, were harder for me, but for some reason, I could remember the poems. This is one I never forgot. I knew I could be like this poem if I just tried my hardest, and I always did.

* * *

I'm Much Too Big for A Fairy
by Leroy F. Jackson

I'm much too big for a fairy,
And much too small for a man
But this is true:
Whatever I do,
I'll do it the best I can.

* * *

We also had music time in our class. I loved to sing and still remember some of the songs. I always feel nostalgic when I think of them. We learned the song Swanee River, and for some reason I've never understood, I felt sad when we sang it. If I hear it or even think of it, especially the chorus, I get a sad feeling inside.

* * *

Swanee River Chorus

All the world is sad and dreary
Everywhere I roam
O dear ones, how my heart grows weary
Far from the old folks at home

* * *

I have come to believe my sadness was and is because the song talks about the world being sad and dreary everywhere I roam and how my heart grows weary. They were all-too-familiar feelings to me as I was always roaming around places by myself.

When I was a kid, parents went alone to the school Open House. I was always afraid my teacher would say something bad about me, but I never heard anything bad when my mom came home. My dad never went. He was usually out drinking. Once my mother came home and I heard her tell a neighbor that my teacher said I had a hard time learning some stuff, but that I tried the hardest in the class. When I heard that, it felt like she knew me; like she really could see how hard I was trying. In my mind, it meant she knew I was not just a bad kid. She will never know how her comment lifted a broken child's heart. I believe my love of poetry began in that class. I think of her often, and thank God for her being a caring teacher who could see the real me. We never know how something we say can hurt or help a person. When she told my mother I tried the hardest, she could not have known it would reach my ears and lift me up the way it did.

Three

Growing up in the project was hard. It was a tough place to live and I hated it there. I had to learn to take care of myself. I was living in a world full of unlovely people, which included my mother and my older sister. I hated older boys as well as they were always trying to get me to do nasty stuff. I avoided them at all costs. I had to be able to feel what I couldn't see.

I learned to stay sharp and move fast. I never walked up or down a flight of steps, I ran. I never took the elevator unless a grownup I knew was getting on it. Elevators were not safe places to be. Neither were hallways. Whether going in or out, you did it as quickly as you could. It was much safer to be outside than inside because you were less likely to be trapped outside. Outside, there was room to run. Strange people hung out in the halls. Unless you were part of a group hanging out, you moved quickly coming in and going out. But even being in a group did not always mean you were safe. When I was five- or six-years old, my older sister Karen got grabbed one afternoon in the hall playing with some other kids. A guy in a trench coat picked her up and ran down the stairs with her. She was kicking and screaming. He dropped her and somehow her leg got cut. The police had to come and talk to all the kids about what the guy looked like and stuff. I was not in the group when she got grabbed, but I was there when the police came to talk to all the kids. It made me even more fearful. I was not a kid who would hang out in the halls at all. I was alone most of the time and knew they were not safe. I quickly became street smart. I learned to never let others know I was afraid or see me cry. I became fearless, and as tough as nails on the outside, but inside, I felt like a terrified little bird that wanted to fly away. I usually used the back door because I knew it was safer than the front where the mailboxes were. You never knew who would be hanging around the mailboxes. My grandmother lived in the same project for a while and when I went into her building, I had to use the front door. One time I went in the building I was afraid of a guy who was at the mailbox. It seemed like he was pretending to be looking for mail, but he didn't have a key, so I backed out of the building and ran home.

On Sunday mornings after church, I used to go to the store for a couple of neighbors to get them the Sunday paper. One Sunday, my sister Linda decided to go with me. We just collected the last of the money from the lady who lived on the fourth floor when we heard a voice yell, "Who's over there?" around the other side of the hall. It was a man's voice and we knew a man didn't live on that side. The hall was U shaped. We were on the right side of the U and the voice came from the left side. We were paralyzed with fear. We knocked on the door of our mother's friend Alice's apartment, the one where my mother spent her days commiserating with her over my dad's escapades. Arleen, her daughter, came to the door and we told her about the man on the other side who yelled to us. We told her we were afraid and asked her to let us in. I was stunned when she said no. Linda and I were crying now and kept knocking on the door and pleading to be let in, but someone on the other side kept saying no. I could not believe they would not let us in. We were downright terrified and afraid to move. Finally, Arleen came out and told me to give her the money and that she would go to the store for me. Then the three of us ran down the stairs. As we ran I could hear the footsteps of whoever had been in the hallway right behind us. We flew down those stairs. Linda and I ran into our apartment while

Arleen continued on down the stairs to the store.

No one would even listen to us when we got inside. I am sixty-five years old now, and can say without a doubt, I have never been more afraid than I was that day. This happened a couple of years after Karen was grabbed in the hallway. That Sunday morning was one of the many things my sister Linda asked me about when we were adults. She said she could never forget that morning. For her, too, it was the most frightening experience of her life. She talked about how nobody seemed to care how afraid we were, and how, when we got into our apartment, it was like it was no big deal. She said it hurt deeply that nobody understood how traumatized we were by what happened.

* * *

In order to understand my day to day living, I think it is important to understand how my family operated. Addiction is a family disease. When an alcoholic, or any addict is part of the family, everyone is affected. Each person must cope with the effects and deal with the problems it causes inside and outside the family, and each family member typically adopts their own coping strategies.

The patterns family members generally follow have been extensively studied, but they are not set in stone. They are basic strategies families with addiction often adopt to cope. I learned this at the Caron Foundation as well as from other reading I did at the time I was seeking help. However, I am by no means an expert about addiction or codependence. I can only speak about my own experience in the hope it might help others. Also, there are several books interested readers can find on the subject.

I will do my best to explain, in the simplest way I can, what these roles are and how they operate within the family.

Alcoholic: The person with the addiction. Their lives revolve around their addiction. They cope with life through avoiding dealing with their feelings by numbing out from them using whatever substance they are addicted to. This was my father.

Enabler/Codependent: Usually the addict's spouse who is often in denial about the addict's problem. They tend to make excuses for the addict's behavior. They can be controlling as well as angry and self-righteous. The word martyr comes to mind. This was my mother.

Hero: Usually the first born; the responsible one. They can become overachievers and perfectionists. They are often seen as the good child. They can be very helpful to parents. They get lots of praise in the family. This was my older sister Karen and my brother Rick.

Scapegoat: Usually the second born. This is the child who gets blamed for everything that is going on. This child, who is rejected by the parents, usually acts out by being angry and defiant. This child is often thought of as the black sheep of the family. This was me and my brother Stephen. I began as my mother's scapegoat, but in time, both parents blamed me. My brother Stephen was mostly my father's scapegoat. My mother tended to baby Stephen, but my dad was hard on him.

Mascot: This person is the family clown, the funny one, who relieves the tension with comedy. We didn't have one in our family other than to say we all played this role at different times. My father was a huge joker. He was pretty much the funny one in the family.

Lost Child: The quiet invisible child who avoids attention. They tend to be very isolated and withdrawn. This was my sisters Linda's and Paula's role. They both were very lost.

The above said, children in a family can often play each roll at different periods throughout their childhood, but in my family, we all pretty much stuck with our main roles at home. When I was away from home, like at my aunt's house, I took the hero roll. In school, I was kind of a loner who didn't get into trouble. Also, I was not the typical scapegoat in the sense of attracting attention away from my family. That was my bother Stephen's role. He became addicted as a teen and got in trouble with the law.

Alcoholic homes can be unpredictable and chaotic. That was how my house was. There did not seem to be any break from the daily consequences of my father's drinking. My mother was being hurt constantly, physically and emotionally. She was either crying or mad and yelling. She was completely overwhelmed by her emotions, so much so, she was unable to see, let alone help her children with *their* emotions. We were all basically on our own emotionally. She did things like cook and clean for us and if we got sick, she would take care of us, but it ended there. If we were fighting, she would never ask what happened. She didn't care. She just wanted us to be quiet and not bother her. Whoever she could hear was the one who got punished. Usually, it was me.

My mother was completely consumed by my father's behavior. It was all she ever talked about and her pain was palpable. I would hear her cry a lot at night when we were in bed. During the day she would seek out comfort and understanding from her friends.

She and the upstairs neighbor were friends throughout the years we lived in the project. She spent as much time as possible at her house, to the point of almost never being home. That was not an exaggeration. It may seem like an extreme statement, but it's true. One story my mother told me many times was how I wanted her attention one day when I was around five years old. We lived right under her friend. Apparently, I went downstairs and proceeded to climb out the window and hang there by my fingertips until she came down and pulled me inside. That was one of her examples of how selfish I was. I don't remember the window incident, but I do remember being told all the time by her friend that my mother was in Sing Sing. It was a standard statement when I knocked at the door. I think they did the same thing at times to some of my siblings. For a time, I thought Sing Sing was the Chinese laundry up the street. I went to that laundry many times looking for her. It took more than a few times for me to catch on that saying my mother was in Sing Sing meant she was not going to let me talk to my mother. I guess that is why I hung out the window. Since I don't remember the incident, I have no idea what I had to talk to her about, but it must have been pretty important to my five-year-old brain. I certainly would not have dared to do that if it wasn't. But I can still remember how desperate and alone I used to feel when someone would answer the door and not let me see my mother. I hated being told my mother was in Sing Sing, and felt hopeless and angry that there was no way to reach her.

One really bad thing about my mother being upstairs was she left my older sister Karen in charge of the house and the little kids. Since she was the Hero, she did all she could to help my mother with things like house cleaning and caring for the younger kids. She was babysitting when she was only nine years old. Of course, I had no intention of letting her boss me, which put the two of us at odds all the time. She was trying to keep the house together. We didn't have nice furniture, so my mother always had sheets covering the couch and chairs so they would look decent. I would come in the house, plop down on a chair and Karen would lose it, telling me I needed to sit on the floor if I wanted to watch TV. Of course, her being who she was, she wanted everything to stay perfect. All I wanted was to sit on the couch or chair and watch TV. I had no intention of sitting on the floor and didn't care if the couch got messed up. I figured I could fix it when I got up. We fought like cats and dogs all the time and she would beat the crap out of me. I always felt like I could beat her up, but she was a dirty fighter. She scratched and bit. I punched, not scratched, and could not bring myself to bite. I always wondered how she could sink her teeth into flesh knowing how bad it would hurt someone. I guess it had always been an issue with her. I remember my mother telling me when I was little, Karen would bite me all the time. My mother said she bit Karen a few times to try to teach her not to bite but it never worked.

I hated living in that house. I was always getting hit by someone. Karen would not let me play with the other kids either. Whenever she was not around and my mother was, I got to play with my sister Linda. We would play with our paper dolls and took turns pretending we were singers. We would put the record player on and play my mother's Patsy Cline records. I still love to listen to the old songs. They bring me back to the few good memories I have with me and my sister Linda.

My mother and father both loved to read, so there were lots of books in our house. When we played paper dolls, we would use the books as dividers to make rooms in our paper-doll house. I loved playing with Linda. She was the only friend I had in the house. But when Karen would catch us playing, she would kick the books down and start fighting with me, which usually made me run out of the house for the rest of the day. I thought it was so hateful of her to not let us play together. We always picked the books up and put them back where they belonged, so there was no good reason other than my sister being mean.

Linda passed away a couple of years ago from ovarian cancer. I loved her dearly. She was my only friend when I was growing up and we remained extremely close. We were only one year apart and when we did play together, we had a blast. I was also the sister Linda depended on to protect her. Whenever she was afraid, she would come to me or wake me if I was sleeping. I used to boost her onto the closet shelf. Then I would climb up there with her. We felt safe on the shelf. Nobody would be able to find us there. As adults, we talked about some of the things that happened when we were young. She would ask me if I remembered this or that. Most stuff I did remember, but some of it only when she reminded me about it. She thanked me once for protecting her when she was young and told me how safe she felt the times I helped her get on the closet shelf.

Linda developed ovarian cancer around 2008. She lost her battle with it in March 2016. I was blessed to be able to be there for her through some of her battles with this horrible disease. My other sisters were as well. It was difficult for all of us when she passed away just eleven weeks after our mother.

* * *

My mother only did the basics for us kids. I guess that was

all she could do. We had little money, so she became very resourceful and could really stretch a buck. She was always looking for a bargain and I inherited her abilities. I am quite resourceful and have learned to look for a deal.

It was hard for me to hear my own daughter once tell me that growing up, she always felt bad about some of the clothes I bought for her. She said she would rather have had me pay more for one pair of jeans than try to get more for less. I had no idea she felt that way until she was grown. Sadly, we don't know what we don't know, but oh, how I wish I *had* known. Looking for bargains back then was not as easy as it is today with computers. I never realized how time consuming it was for my mother until I was an adult. I have no idea how she found the time back then, but somehow, she managed. We may not have had the best clothes, but we had them.

In the fourth grade, I remember having two outfits I loved. They were corduroy skirts, one black and one red, and they had striped blouses that went with them, one red, one black. Each had corduroy patches on the elbows that matched the skirts. They were awesome and I loved them. Whenever I see a red or black striped blouse, I remember those two outfits.

Growing up, all we had were the essentials. I remember how excited I was at Christmas when I was eight. My sisters and I got new pajamas with matching cloth slippers from Santa. I felt like a queen with them on.

Me, 8 and Karen, 10 in our new Christmas PJs with matching slippers.

That was the first time I remember having pajamas, which were a luxury.

My mother struggled to keep us in clothes, so we usually slept in undies and tee shirts. There were so many things I saw other kids have that I wished I could have, like a lunch box with a thermos in it, a raincoat, and galoshes to keep my shoes dry. I hated wet feet.

When I was four or five, my grandfather — my father's father — and my step grandmother took me, my older sister Karen, my sister Linda and my brother Rick for the weekend. They took us shopping and bought us new clothes, including new undies and socks. It was so exciting shopping with them. I can still remember the pedal pushers they got for me. They were beautiful and I loved them. They had stripes on the cuffs with a matching striped blouse to go with them. Each of us girls got a couple of pairs. I don't remember what they bought my brother Rick for clothes. We wanted to bring the clothes home, but they told us the clothes were for us to wear when we visited. Unfortunately, I never got to wear them as I did not get to visit them again as a child.

I do remember them buying us toys like coloring books and puzzles. They bought my brother Ricky a huge Lionel Train set. They set it up for him when we got back from the store. I was so happy for Ricky. He was having a wonderful time watching the trains go around and around.

When we were older, there were weekends we visited my grandfather and times he took Karen and I to see the Red Sox. Then I didn't see him again until I was sixteen. I was headed to Logan Airport to fly to visit a friend in Virginia. On the way, I stopped at the cab stand where he worked. I told him I was engaged and wanted him to come to my wedding the next year. He promised he would and true to his word, he came.

Another thing I wished for was that we could all get birthday presents. Our birthdays consisted of a cake my mother made. Sometimes there was ice cream, but not always. There would be candles but not always the right number for our age. It never really felt like a birthday, not like the ones other kids had, especially on TV. I did get a birthday present one time, when I turned seven. On his way home from work, my father got me a pair of yellow electric scissors. I felt so special getting a present from my dad, but I also felt kind of sad because I never saw anybody else get a gift.

As I got older, I was always mad at my father because I

knew he didn't do his best. He was too busy drinking to care about us. I remember I would watch him shaving when I was young. I would see him all dressed up and knew he was going out on the town to have fun. I grew to hate seeing him like that because I knew it was going to be a bad night. I knew that my mother would be hurt and mad.

I had to be especially careful those nights since my mother was already angry when he left the house and it would not take much for her to start with me. Those nights, I could barely fall asleep as I knew I would be waking up to the sound of fighting. Deep in my heart, I blamed him for my mother not being nice to me. I always thought if she was not so mad and hurt all the time, maybe she would not be so mean; that she would not need to talk to her friends so much and would have time to spend with us kids. I don't remember her ever spending time playing with us or doing anything fun at all other than the time she told me about playing ghosts with Karen and me. I know there were times she took us places. Sometimes in the summer, we would walk down to the Green Street Pool. There were also a few times I remember she took us to the Beach on a bus. But all she did was watch us. She didn't participate. I don't remember her ever swimming with us or playing with us on the sand. When we went to the lake with my dad, he would come in the water and play with us. I remember he would pick us up and throw us into the water, but my mother just watched.

* * *

I grew to hate my father as much as I was growing to hate my mother. I was very conflicted in my feelings about my parents. I loved and hated them both. I thought God would surely send me to hell for hating them, but I had heard of purgatory, so I thought I might end up there instead of hell. I thought if by some chance He did decide to send me there, I would be stuck there forever. I knew there would be nobody to pray for me to get to heaven. I didn't think anybody would care where I was. I thought they would all just be happy that I was gone, and there were times I prayed to die. At those times, I was sure they would all be better off if I was gone.

The belief that no one would care where I was never left me for very long. I feared it to the point I would think about some poor soul stuck in purgatory with nobody to pray for them to get to heaven. When I went to bed each night, I would pray for the people there. I would say lots of prayers, then say the first five are for a person close to getting to heaven and please let them in. Then five for someone far away from heaven to get them closer. I did this until I fell asleep most nights. I hoped my praying helped someone like me get to God and that if I died, someone might do the same thing to help me. Maybe if someone prayed like I did, I might get lucky enough to go to heaven.

I didn't know a lot about God, but I knew He hated people being bad. I knew I was bad because a few times, I stole Devil Dogs. But mostly I knew I was bad because my mother told me I was. One of my mother's favorite things to say to me was that I was a bold bitch. I knew being bold was bad, probably the worst thing God hated. One of the songs we sang when I made my First Holy Communion was called *Little White Guest*.

* * *

Little White Guest

You have come to my heart, dearest Jesus,
I am holding You close to my breast;
I'm telling You over and over,
You are welcome, Little White Guest.

I love You, I love You, my Jesus,
O please do not think I am bold;
Of course, You must know that I love You,
But I am sure that You like to be told.

I'll whisper, "I love You, my Jesus,"
And ask that we never may part;
I love You, O kind, loving Jesus
And press You still nearer my heart.

And when I shall meet You in Heaven,
My soul then will lean on Your breast;
And You will recall our fond meetings,
When You were my Little White Guest.

* * *

I remember singing that song. I would shake because I didn't
want to be bold but knew I was and knew I was doomed. After
all, they said God let His own son Jesus die, which I didn't
understand because they also said Jesus was perfect. I was very
afraid of God.

They also said we were supposed to honor our father and
mother. I had no idea what honor meant, but I was pretty sure I
wasn't very good at it. The nuns said God could forgive
people's sins. I was not sure *how* forgiveness happened, but a
small part of me hoped He would forgive me because the nuns
said He loved us.

The day before I made my First Holy Communion, I had to
go to confession where I told the priest some of my sins. I told
him I stole three times, lied three times, and that I was bold to
my mother three times. I knew I was bold way more than that
but was afraid to tell him, so I stuck with the three for
everything. I knew I did other bad stuff but thought what I told
him would be good enough. I have no idea where I came up
with the number three.

I felt clean as I came out of church that afternoon. I *never*
before felt that good. But then I saw a kid from the
neighborhood on the church steps. I don't remember if he did
something or if I just decided to call him a name, but I did, and
remember looking back at the church, feeling bad. I felt like I
could not go back into the church and confess what I just did,
so I walked home feeling lower than the gutter. I felt deep
shame and didn't know what to do since I was supposed to get
Jesus the next day. I felt dirty from cursing at the kid and Jesus
was pure, but I was stuck. I couldn't tell anyone. I know I told
God I was sorry, but I was afraid of what might happen to me
getting Jesus after cursing.

My mother woke me early the next morning. I looked beautiful and felt like a princess all in white with my hair curled and combed. My mother and her family were all making a fuss about me and I felt special for the first time in my life. My mothers' aunts were taking pictures, which was rare. It was an amazing day for me until I had to go up to the altar, kneel, and let the priest put that little white Host in my mouth. I felt sick to my stomach thinking about the day before but knew there was nothing I could do. As I walked back to the pew, I felt like I would choke on the Host. I kneeled and prayed that God would not be mad at me. I was sorry for cursing at the boy and for letting Jesus body and blood get in me while I was dirty from cursing. Despite how I felt, I somehow managed to let it go and enjoy the day with my mother and aunts. We went to my mother's father's house, where my mother's paternal grandmother lived. I vaguely remember seeing her that one time in my life.

* * *

I would like to say there were many good times in our house, but they were so few and far between, they didn't count much.

Christmas would always be nice; seeing the presents Santa brought us under the tree. There was always stuff not wrapped, like a carriage, a truck, or a doll highchair with a baby doll in it. That was exciting to see. But after the gifts were opened, my mother would put them in piles under the tree, a pile for each child. Then she and my father would spend the rest of the day yelling at us for going under the tree to take something to play with.

Other than the fact that Santa brought me some nice things, mostly I hated Christmas. The night before was always hard for me because my mother was usually up alone crying and looking out the window a lot. I hated it and felt sorry for her. I was always wishing my father would come home early, but I don't think he ever did.

We used to have the lights that looked like candles in the

windows. Some would have five lights, some three, and some only had one. They made me feel sad. Despite the nice parts, Christmas was a sad time of year to me. To this day, seeing those lights in a window makes me feel sad.

One fun thing I remember was my mother always let us kids break up the bread for the stuffing. She would make us wash our hands before we could help her with it. I loved stuffing. I hated the vegetables she cooked on Christmas and Thanksgiving, the squash, turnips, and carrots, but I loved the cranberry sauce, potatoes, stuffing, and gravy. Turkey I could take or leave and I was not a pie eater, so I didn't care about that either. My mother would always make us all eat a little of all the vegetables, but what she called a little was always more than I could choke down.

* * *

One Thanksgiving, my father saw us kids all moping around. He asked us why we were not happy. He said we should be feeling thankful because it was Thanksgiving. He didn't understand why we were all so upset so I spoke up and said, "How can we be thankful when we have to eat stuff we hate." That day when we sat down for dinner, he told my mother to leave us alone from now on and not make us eat stuff we didn't like. It was great that day! Of course, when he was not home, she would make us eat the veggies, like it or not. But it was fine since I had a deal with my older sister—she ate my carrots and I ate her spinach. I don't know why we never got caught.

That was about all Karen and I ever agreed on. We were as different as night and day, like fire and ice. At the time, I never understood why she hated me, but today, I do—I threw a monkey wrench into everything she was trying to do. She hated me cursing and fighting with my mother. Her very existence was to be helpful to my mother and I was the exact opposite. I never cared about what my mother or Karen wanted. I was always just screaming about how unfair my mother was. Since I was the scapegoat, I thought I could clearly see all that was going on. As it turned out, I did see much clearly, but certainly not all.

For years after I rejected my father, I would often yell at my mother to divorce him. I'm not sure I fully understood what that meant, but I was tired of all of it. If he didn't live with us, I believed my mother would not be so hurt and mad all the time, and maybe she would be nicer, especially to me. I wasn't positive, though, since she would always tell me I was just like him. Although there were good parts of him, I knew she was talking about the bad parts, like the screaming and yelling he did when he was drunk. She was right, because I was a yeller like him. Sometimes, I would sit alone outside and think about the things my mother said to me and wish I could just die. There were times I felt such self-loathing I would punish myself by slapping my own face. Or I would stay outside in the freezing cold until I could not stand it anymore.

There were times I would think about something that happened and just be angry at my mother or father for not listening to me. I would go over and over what happened in my head making sure I could remember it. I was afraid if I couldn't remember it clearly, they would convince me it really was all my fault and I could not let them do that to me. I would never give in to the things they said. I would sometimes feel like I would go crazy. Those were the times I would repeat to myself, over and over, what actually happened. It was knowing the truth that would help me stay sane.

My mother always reacted badly if you believed you were right about anything. She would try to badger you into agreeing with her, and would get the other kids to help her, but I was never going to agree with any of them. As far as I was concerned, they were all as bad as my mother, though, for the most part, it was my sister Karen when I was young. This caused tremendous conflict with me and my siblings. My mother was masterful at making something look different than it really was. She would say or do something to me that no one else heard and that would get me started. Then she would stand back while I was being treated badly. I was always on the outside looking in. I lived in a house with seven other people, yet I was completely alone. I always just wanted to be part of the family. I wanted her to love me too. What I didn't know was that it might have looked like she loved the other kids, but they were a mess as well, each of us playing the roles, each of us in our own private hell.

There was a part of me that hated my mother. She never listened to me when something happened she just punished me. I didn't know she was not listening to the other kids either. We were all casualties of an alcoholic home, but I had no way of knowing that. I only knew how *my* life was. We were all in pain and desperately in need of love. I didn't know that even as my older sister was being praised all the time, she was deeply hurt and confused.

As I look back, I may have been the lucky one. I could get out of the house to escape what was happening. I would go outside all the time and seek out things that made me feel good. I joined the Girl Scouts once. I would go to the Neighborhood House. I played the triangle there for a while and wanted to take the dance lessons, but didn't have tap shoes, so I would just watch.

In warm weather, I would go to the outdoor fountain sprinklers for children to run through and play in. They had three different ones in the project. They also had people who taught us how to make stuff like key chains with gimp. They had different projects we could do and were nice to us. I really liked nice people and gravitated toward them. I still do. I'm convinced I could not have survived my childhood without seeking people who treated me well. Of course, not all the people were nice, and there were times I found myself in situations I didn't understand, but being street smart usually helped me avoid most bad stuff.

* * *

I was always doing something, usually alone, whether in the house or outside somewhere. Later this being alone would get me in trouble. I would find myself in situations I had no idea how to handle. Once I got stuck at the roller rink when a friend decided she was going to go babysit for someone close to the rink rather than have her dad pick us up and bring us back to Dover. I was left there alone with no ride so I talked to a person I knew who said her brother would get me to Dover. I left the roller rink and went to her house to catch the ride only to learn her brother decided he would have his friend drive me. That friend drove to a wooded area and tried to make me have sex with him. I would not so he slapped me around and threw me out of the car. By that time, it was late at night and I had to walk home alone in the dark. Thank God the wooded area was not far from where I lived.

One thing I did as much as I could was visit my aunt Joan, my father's sister, whenever she was living close enough for me to walk to her house. *She* loved me and I knew it. She would let me stay up late on Saturday night and watch the late show *Chillerama*. It showed horror movies and was very scary and I loved it. My aunt made ice cream floats with coffee ice cream and orange soda for us before we watched the movie. Everything at my aunt's house was better. The Tooth Fairy was even richer there. She left at least fifteen cents sometimes a quarter for a tooth. You could get a lot for fifteen cents then — Yankee Doodle cupcakes *and* a bag of Wise Potato Chips. If you got a quarter, you could add a Pepsi. At my house, the fairy only left a nickel. If I thought my tooth was going to come out, I would do my best to keep it in until I could spend the night at my aunt's. She would also let me help her do stuff like dishes and laundry. I can still remember her putting the clothes through the hand ringer on the old-type washing machine. She would not let me do that part, saying it was too dangerous. But after the laundry was washed, we would wheel it in the carriage to the laundromat to dry it all. My aunt trusted me enough to leave me there to watch them. She would put the clothes into the dryer and go home. When they were dry, I would take them out and fold them as best I could for a seven-year-old, then wheel them back to her house.

I worshiped her. There was nothing I would not do to help

her. It felt good being appreciated and allowed to help. Sometimes, my aunt would send me to the store to get her some comic books. She loved Archie and when I went to the store, she always gave me a nickel for myself. One time, on the way to the store, I got the skin on my head split open. I was running with my head down. My head was always down because I was sensitive to the sunlight and at times got sun blindness. A teenager on a bike was on the sidewalk and ran right into me. It really hurt but I continued to the store to get the comic books. The guy at the register was upset when he saw me. He asked me what happened and told me I was bleeding badly from my head. I was afraid when he said that, so I touched where my head got hit and my hand was covered with blood, which scared me. I ran back to my aunt's house and my uncle took me to the emergency room at Boston City Hospital. The doctor said I needed stitches and was about to put them in when another doctor came into the room and told the first doctor that he didn't have to stitch everything, that he could use butterfly stitches on me.

I was happy about that. I knew what butterfly stitches were and knew they didn't hurt. My mother had put butterfly stiches on my eyebrow one time when Karen threw a spoon at me and split above my left eye on the corner of my eyebrow. It was the only time I ever saw Karen get in trouble and only because my mother saw her throw the spoon at me for no good reason. I was happy she got a spanking for it.

* * *

I loved my aunt and being at her house so much, I would sometimes feel guilty. Though I did love my mother, it felt like I was betraying her by loving my aunt as much as I did. I vividly remember one time my aunt was bringing me home after being at her house for a few days. Just before I got out of the car, I looked at my uncle and her, then at the building where I lived. I wanted to go home because I missed my mother. But there was also a part of me that hurt having to leave my aunt. I had a huge lump in my throat. It hurt so bad, I felt like I was going to die. I never before felt that bad. It was the worst feeling in the world. I am not someone who gets a lump in my throat often — only a few times in my life — but that was the first time.

Looking back at those times, I can see how lucky I was that I could get away from the chaos at home while the other kids were stuck in it. I think about my sister Karen, who was so responsible. She was just a kid like me but she was taking care of the house and the kids all the time. She never really got to go out to play and do stuff because she was always in the house watching the little kids, even when she was just a kid herself. What I envied as a child I don't envy now. I find myself praying for my siblings often. I remember how it was. What I didn't understand then, I understand now. What a sad lot we were. This was not happening because my parents were bad people. I can't express this enough. These were the ravages of alcoholism and codependence.

Four

We moved from 940 Parker Street when I was nine years old because my mom had my baby sister, Paula, who was now two years old, and now that we had six children, we were eligible for a four-bedroom apartment. We moved to 24 Heath Street, which was in the same project and not far from where we had been living. You could see our old building from our new one.

I didn't want to move there for two reasons. First, moving put us in a different school zone and I would have to go to a new school. Second, a blond girl who was older and way bigger than me and I was afraid of her.

I was small for my age. All of us kids were. We took after our mother who was very petite, just four feet eleven inches tall. This girl was a giant compared to me and she was mean. The first time I met her, she told me she was going to beat me up. The day we moved in I was terrified to run into her, so I hung around the house until my parents told me to go out and play. As it turned out, she was all talk. Of that, I was glad, because other than not wanting to change schools and being afraid of her, there was a lot to look forward to.

Since we had four bedrooms, I would now be sharing a room with only Karen. Linda and my baby sister Paula were now sharing a room and my brothers Rick and Stephen still shared a bedroom. Most amazing was that the double beds we used to sleep in were thrown out and we each got our own bed.

It was such a surprise! No one told me we were getting new beds.

I remember going to bed the night we moved in. It felt strange climbing into bed alone, but it also felt wonderful and thinking nobody could steal the blankets anymore. I had such a good feeling as I snuggled up under the new top sheet and blanket. We never had two sheets on our bed before or a pillow. I remember feeling so safe and peaceful. Also, there was no foul smell of our old pee-stained mattress. I can still remember how blessed I felt that night as I drifted off to sleep.

As far as the girl who threatened to beat me up, I remained afraid of her the whole time we lived there. She really was a mean one and she ended up being our babysitter. She was better than the boys, but not great. She bossed everyone, even me. She used to bury us in the snow. I am not talking about just a little bit of snow on us. She would put so much snow on us that we could not get out. It was scary. She would leave just a little hole for our nose and mouth so we could breathe and we were stuck in it until she unburied us. I never wanted to go outside that winter even though I usually loved playing in the snow and building snowmen and forts as well as sliding down small hills on cardboard.

That Christmas she told us we were going to put on a show for our parents. She had records and made us learn songs. It was kind of fun other than the songs she chose for me to sing. I didn't want to sing them, especially *Nuttin' for Christmas*. My mother loved that she gave me that song. She said it fit me well. Everybody laughed when I sang it. I felt ashamed and it made me mad that everybody thought I was bad.

* * *

I hated the Charles Bulfinch School. My teacher was a mean person and I knew she didn't like me. That year, I got head lice and everyone in my class made fun of me. I wanted to just die knowing they all knew I got them. They started calling me buggy Bennett. I was not dirty. We took a bath and shampooed our hair every single night. I didn't know how I got the damn bugs, but I felt so embarrassed at school.

My mother did what she was supposed to do to get rid of them. She used the special shampoo on our heads and cut our hair short. She also combed through it. That was not the first time we caught them, but it was the first-time people in my school knew I got them. My mother was brutal with combing those combs through our hair. When Aunt Joan helped, she was not rough like my mother.

Once after school, just before we crossed the street, I was talking in line. I figured it was ok since school was over. The teacher told me to be quiet. Of course, I let her know I didn't have to be quiet because school was over and she slapped me right across the face. I ran home and told my mother but she didn't do a thing. I thought she would be mad at the teacher for hitting me but no, she didn't care a bit. She said I probably deserved it. I didn't think I deserved it since we were not even on school property when it happened.

* * *

At first, the new apartment seemed quieter and more peaceful than the old one. The building was only three stories and stood on the corner of the street, giving it a more subdued appearance. 940 Parker was seven stories high and surrounded by other seven story buildings just like it. As a small child it was overwhelming being surrounded by such big buildings.

There was no elevator to have to deal with and fewer people going in and out of the building, so it felt a bit safer at first, with only twelve apartments instead of the twenty-eight at Parker Street, but there were other differences between the two apartments that were not good.

On Parker Street, I could hear beer bottles breaking under my bedroom window at night and was always afraid until my dad got home, but the adults didn't hang around outside during the day. Other than children getting into squabbles, it was mostly quiet until sunset. On Heath Street, adults hung around outside day and night and there was a lot of violence during the day while children were still outside. This was the place my friend's father was beaten up when a group of teens pulled up in front of our building at dinner time and used a wine bottle to knock his teeth out.

It was the place where the lady with the meat fork concealed under her coat, who lived in the unit below us, was looking for my mother and telling people she was going to kill her. And it was here my father got his leg cut open by a group of black teens while he was changing his tire.

My sisters and I found a dead body in a car one time on our way to church. A guy was on the floor in the back of a car sort of leaning against the door. One of my sisters ran home to tell my dad who called the police. The police and fire department came. I remember they broke a window to reach the lock and open the door. I knew he was dead because after they put him on a stretcher, then they put a sheet over his face just like in the movies. I hated everything about living on Heath Street.

I was much more afraid living there than our other apartment. I didn't know I could be more afraid than I had been. It seemed like a different world to me.

I don't know why there was more violence here and often wondered if it had something to do with things going on in our country during that year. I know there was a lot of civil unrest during the 1960s and we lived at 24 Heath Street from the summer of 1963 through the summer of 1964.

We moved out of the project completely toward the end of August, 1964.

* * *

Years later, I asked my mother why we moved out of the project. She told me one day I came home and described in detail to my father how I saw a guy stick a knife in someone and twist it. At that point, I guess my dad told her we were moving and to start packing. I don't remember the incident, and asked her many times throughout the years if she was sure it was me not one of the other kids. She was positive it was me. Again, I have no memory of it, but I have always been afraid of knives. I don't keep them anyplace I can see them, and never use much more than a steak knife.

We moved from Heath Street to Sachem Street when I was ten. I don't remember what the number was, but it was up the street from Peter Bent Brigham Hospital, which is now called Brigham and Women's. It was a nice neighborhood. The apartment was nice, so different than those in the project. The building was wood frame, not brick. It was three stories and we lived on the top floor. We always seemed to live on the third floor. We had a porch at the back of our apartment, and a back yard for the little kids to play in.

I used to roller-skate up and down the street on the sidewalk and hang out with some other kids and play hopscotch and things like that. It was the coldest place we ever lived. I remember being cold at night trying to sleep. But there was no violence I can remember, and I didn't feel afraid all the time anymore. The only times I was ever afraid here had to do with school. I hated going to school in Roxbury. I went to the Farragut School. There were a lot of boys in my class and they would beat up me and my sister on the way to school and on the way home. I remember hiding under porches on the way to school if I saw any of the boys in my class. On the way home it was harder because they followed us after the bell rang. These boys were worse than the ones in the project. When I got in fights in the project it was usually one on one. I was never attacked by a group. But in Roxbury, there were usually at least two of them. I was very afraid going to that school. When I broke my arm, they decided to leave me alone when they found out my cast hurt, and I was not afraid to swing it. Again, I wonder how much of the fighting with the kids during that time could have been due to the civil unrest during 1964. It was during 1964 that the *Civil Rights Act*, which outlawed discrimination based on Race, Color, Religion, Sex, or National Origin was signed into law. People fought hard for that.

Living on Sachem Street, I missed going to my old church, Blessed Sacrament, on Sundays as well as my catechism classes on Mondays. I had gone to that church my whole life. Now, we all had to go to one which was closer. We called it the Mission

Hill Church, but I believe the real name was Our Lady of
Perpetual Help. It was the church where Senator Edward
Kennedy's funeral was held. One day I was visiting a friend in
2009 and she had the TV on watching his funeral. When I saw
the church, it sent shivers down my spine. I remembered going
to it the whole time we lived on Sachem Street. It felt weird
seeing it on TV and brought back so many memories of
Sundays walking to and from the church with my siblings. My
friend was surprised I felt such a strong connection to it. I think
I have always felt a strong connection to everywhere in Boston
since that is where I began my life. My childhood memories all
started there. I still have family in Jamaica Plain. I also have
family in Foxborough, Sharon, and other areas in and around
Boston.

There were no cockroaches here on Sachem. That was
something we always had in the project. My mother used to
say everybody in the project had them. She would get the
exterminator, but it never really got rid of them. It seemed to
me that all calling the exterminator did was stink-up the house.
I hated the smell of what they used, but don't think the roaches
minded it because they didn't go away. My mother said it was
because not everyone got their apartment exterminated. Mom
always left the bathroom light on in case we had to get up in
the middle of the night to pee. If you turned a light on at night,
the roaches would run like hell back to wherever it was they
lived when people were around. I hated cockroaches. They
were disgusting.

I got my first pair of eyeglasses when we lived there. I knew
I needed them because in school, I had a hard time seeing the
blackboard, but I was not looking forward to the kids making
fun of me. I remember how strange and exciting it felt going
with my parents to get glasses. It was the first time I went
anywhere alone with both of them. First, we saw the eye doctor
at the clinic in the hospital to get the prescription. Then we
went to Dudley Street to pick out the glasses. The following
Saturday, we returned to pick them up. I felt so special to be
with them and can still remember walking around Dudley

Street holding both their hands feeling so happy inside. My dad and I both loved hotdogs, so we stopped at a five and dime after the appointments and had a hot dog and chips. Summer was not quite over and both Saturday afternoons were warm sunny days I will always hold dear in my memory.

The glasses were light blue cat style and I hated them. I got made fun of by my sisters and brothers. They called me four eyes. I managed to lose them within a few months. My mother was so mad at me she said she was never going to buy me another pair, which was fine by me. I didn't want them

Mother, Karen (11), Rick (7), Me (9), Linda (8)
Paula (2), Stephen (6)

anyway. Despite not liking or wanting them, I did not lose them on purpose. I did like being able to see better, and felt bad I lost them because I knew they cost my dad a lot of money.

One Saturday, my dad took my sister Karen, me, and Linda to a movie theater, The Rialto in Roslindale. He didn't go into the movie with us. He just dropped us off. He told us he would pick us up when the movie was over. I can still remember what movies we saw – *Gladiator Seven* and *Children of the Dammed*. Those were the days when theaters showed two movies, a news reel, and a cartoon or two for one admission. You could spend a whole afternoon there.

When my dad picked us up, he said we could go to the movies on Saturdays from now on but we would have to take the streetcar. Then he showed us where the streetcar stopped down the street from the theater and where we could pick it up not far from our house. The following Saturday, he gave my older sister money for us to go, with some extra for popcorn and drinks. Then he dropped us off down the street from our house at the streetcar stop. Linda was nine, I was ten, and Karen was twelve. He told Linda and me that Karen was the boss and we better listen to her or we would not get to go again. It was so much fun going to the movies. Karen was not bossy when we went and we all had a blast together. We went to the movies many times after that. I don't have a lot of good memories of my dad when I was young, so I cherish that one a lot.

Another memory I cherish is one where my mother had to stay in the hospital for a few days. She and my dad were in a car accident. Grandmother Bennett had a boyfriend who had a back problem. He asked my mother what they gave her for her pain. When she told him, he asked for one of the pills and she gave him one. Later, he told her that the pills weren't very strong; that they were like water. He said she should tell the doctor the pills didn't work well because they weren't strong enough. Apparently, when she told the doctor, he put her in the hospital right away. She ended up staying for three days.

My father took care of us kids and I thought he was so much fun. One afternoon, he asked us if we would like him to make us grilled cheese with bacon sandwiches and tomato soup for lunch. I was amazed he knew how to cook. He fixed it for us and it was delicious. It was the best lunch I ever had. The weird thing is, I don't care for tomato soup, but that day it was so good. I think it was so good because my father took the time to ask us if we would like him to fix it, then he ate it with us. That was the first time I remember having bacon with grilled cheese and I love it to this day. For me it's a comfort food. My dad was always so nice to us kids. When we were adults, Linda asked me if I remembered that day. Although I was only around five, I remembered it fondly.

When we were young, my dad was, for the most part, easy-going around us kids. He did not like to spank us. I only remember a few spankings and they were group spankings, which meant something happened, like who broke the record player, and nobody would fess up. Then he would make us line up in the hallway, have us come into the room one at a time, put us over his knee, and give us one or two taps on the butt. It never really hurt but we would all stand in the hallway crying and carrying on as if we were going to the gallows. Looking back, it was kind of funny.

He never wanted to discipline us and was not a big hitter. When we lived at 940 Parker Street, we all would fool around when we went to bed. Then we would hear what we thought was our brothers getting the belt. When it stopped, Dad would come into our room and ask if we heard what our brothers just got. Then he would tell us that if we didn't stop fooling around and go to sleep, we would get the same thing. It turned out he never spanked my brothers. He just stood in the bathroom slapping the belt from side to side on the door frame. Then he would come into our room and pretend the boys just got spanked. Then he would go into the boys' room and pretend the girls got spanked. When I was older, my mother told me about him using that trick when she would send him in to make us stop fooling around.

One time my mother was so mad at me and my older sister she made us stay up until my dad got home. I can still remember sitting on the couch waiting for him to come home. She said we were going to be in big trouble when he got there. I have no idea what we did, but I think she was planning on him spanking us. When he got home, he was shocked to see us up. When we told him why we were up he sent us to bed, then told my mother not to keep us up late like that again. He said he was not going to come home and spank us for something we did earlier in the day.

When my dad was around, my mother never let us hang

around with him. She always sent us outside or to our rooms. It seemed like she didn't want to compete with us for his attention. Most of the time we were in bed when he came home and he was usually gone to work before, we got up, so, we didn't get to see him or spend time with him often. But he didn't work on Sunday mornings so he would be up sometimes. It depended on how late he had been out drinking the night before.

He and my mother would go out most Saturday nights, so they didn't usually fight, and seemed to be happy Sunday morning. Those mornings were great. I would get dressed as quick as I could for church so I could sit and eat my cereal while he was still drinking his coffee. My sisters and brothers did the same thing. We would all be around the table and my dad would sing us silly songs, like the one about bedbugs and roaches having a game of ball.

I was standing on the corner,
Not doing any harm,
Along came a flatfoot
And took me by the arm.

He took me around the corner
Then rang a little bell
Along came a paddy
And took me to my cell.

I woke up in the morning
and looked up at the wall
The bedbugs and the roaches
were playin' a game of ball.

The score was two to nothin'
the bedbugs were ahead
the roaches hit a homerun
That knocked me out of bed.

I went downstairs to breakfast

the toast was old and stale
the coffee tastes like tobacco juice
in the Charles Street County Jail.

I have no idea who wrote it and there are many variations.

He also sang a song called *Mairzy Doats*, but his lyrics were a little different at the beginning.

I know a ditty, nutty as a fruitcake
Goofy as a goon, and silly as a loon
Some call it pretty, others call it crazy
But they all sing this tune:

Mairzy doats and dozy doats and liddle lamzy divey
A kiddley divey too, wouldn't you?
Oh! Mairzy doats and dozy doats and liddle lamzy divey
A kiddley divey too, wouldn't you?

If the words sound queer and funny to your ear,
a little bit jumbled and jivey
Sing "Mares eat oats and does eat oats
and little lambs eat ivy"

Oh! Mares eat oats and does eat oats
and little lambs eat ivy
A kiddle eat ivy too, wouldn't you-oo?
A kiddle eat ivy too, wouldn't you?

He would also sing our favorite, *The Preacher and the Bear* by George Fairman. There are a lot of versions of that song. The version my dad sang was the one sung by Phil Harris. My dad sang it better though. Hands down, he sang it better than any version I have heard. He even won a few talent contests singing it. My dad would tell us silly jokes those mornings as well. We would all sit at the table listening until my mother would give us the sign it was time to leave for church.

I didn't mind going to church, but I really didn't want to go the days my dad was up because I wanted to spend more time with him. Looking back, those mornings were an oasis for our thirsty little souls.

Unfortunately, he was not around much. He was either at work or drinking. But there were many times he was not around because he was in the hospital. There were a few years he seemed to be accident prone and would end up in the hospital with some injury or sickness. I know one time he always laughed about was when his boss was standing on a platform talking with him, saying, "Bennett you seem to be accident prone." Just then, a truck drove by and a large piece of wood flew out of the back of the truck, hit my dad right on the head, and knocked him out. He got a concussion and was in the hospital a few days. He was out of work for a few weeks. His boss told him he would not have believed it if he had not seen it with his own eyes. Another time, when a power jack malfunctioned, and something fell on his foot and crushed it, he was hospitalized for quite a while. There were also times he was hospitalized because he was alcohol sick. These hospitalizations happened before we moved to Sachem Street, when we were still in the project.

My mother would take me to the hospital with her because she was afraid to take the subway alone at night. She was afraid of the Boston Strangler. I guess with me being with her, she felt safer. I was too young to visit my dad so I would wait in the waiting room until visiting hours were over. I was bored to death at the hospital, but I never complained or said a word about it because I loved traveling with my mom on the subway. She would talk to me a little bit on the way down and back, but once we moved to Sachem Street, I didn't get to go with her anymore.

Not long after we moved there, Dad got very sick. He had hepatitis and they thought he was going to die. He was in the hospital for about six months. I heard mom talking to my grandmother one time on the phone. She told my gram she might want to go see my dad because he might not make it. I decided I should go see him, so one day after my mother left for the hospital, I walked to it, determined to find a way to see my dad. He had been gone longer than ever before and I really missed him and was afraid I would never see him again. I walked into the hospital and asked the lady at the desk what room Dick Bennett was in. I told her he was my father and I came to see him. When she asked me how old I was and I told her I was ten, she said I could not see him because to visit you had to be at least eleven years old. I left the hospital and cried all the way home.

While we lived on Sachem Street, my brother Stephen broke his elbow so badly he needed an operation to fix it. Mother had to leave him at the hospital for two days. When he came home, he told us that they put bug spray on something and put in on his face. I suppose it was ether. About two weeks after he got his cast off, I broke my right wrist. I was jumping off a fence and landed right on my hand which caused my wrist to break. I remembered what my brother Stephen said they did to him and how he had to stay in the hospital. The thought of me staying in the hospital terrified me. I was not going to let that happen, no matter what. They gave me stuff to put me to sleep so they could set my arm, but I had no intention of closing my eyes and I fought the drugs like crazy. My mother told me the doctor said he gave me enough to knock a horse out and that he couldn't give me anything else.

I cried when they set my arm and kept telling my mother not to tell anyone. The doctor told me it was okay to cry and to stop apologizing. He said I should just close my eyes and sleep. That was not going to happen. I knew if I went to sleep, they would keep me there, so I stayed awake, and after my arm was set, they let me leave with my mother. It was about three in the morning, so she called a cab to bring us home. When I relaxed in the cab, the drugs took effect. I don't remember getting home and only remember bits and pieces of the next day.

Mom had to bring me back to the hospital at 9 AM, just six hours after we got home, so they could x-ray my wrist again, but we could not take the bus because I could not stay awake. She had to call my Uncle Lee to bring us. I remember they put me in a wheelchair because I was unable to walk and I barely remember the x-ray or leaving the hospital. I do remember being in my mother's bed, the one where she had beat my dad with a clothes rack. My sister was making fun of me because I could not wake up. She was pulling my hair and being mean laughing at me and there was nothing I could do. I was so drugged I slept until the next morning.

My cast was on for nearly six months. The doctor laughed as the cast was removed because a bunch of quarters fell on the table. The cast went from my fingertips to my underarm and my arm was bent. I thought when I threw the quarters in it, I would be able to shake them out when I wanted to, but I was not able to get them past the bend in my arm so there they stayed until the cast was removed. I forgot I put them in there and was as surprised as the doctor when they hit the table. My arm was very skinny and I remember thinking it looked funny. The doctor told me it had atrophied because I had not used it for such a long time but it would be okay once the muscle had time to perk itself up.

My father got out of the hospital just after I turned eleven and we moved away from there at the beginning of summer. I was glad. I would not have liked another winter there. It was so cold at night, I had a hard time sleeping. Plus, I hated the school and was so tired of being scared and getting beat up all the time. It was not that I got beat up because I couldn't take care of myself, but it was hard to defend yourself with two people hitting you. I could always hold my own with just one, even when they were bigger, and they were always bigger.

Five

The year I turned eleven, we moved to 85 Rossmore Road in a nice neighborhood in Jamaica Plain where my mother's family lived. Her aunt Barbara lived across the street from us. Her sister, Ester, lived one street over with her husband Bob. They had three kids Bobby, Larry, and Donna. It was the first time I would be living near a cousin who was only few years younger than me. It was also not far from Lee Street, where my mother grew up and my grandfather still lived. It was only a few streets away from us, and there were other family members of hers I didn't know very well who lived in that area.

It was a very tranquil, predominantly white middle class neighborhood. There was not a trace of the racial tension I lived with for so long. It was quiet and peaceful—the best place we ever lived—and I was so happy we moved there. Dad bought mom a new bedroom and living room set. They were beautiful. She never had new furniture for her bedroom or living room and she was over the moon and walking on clouds for months. Mom liked stuff to look nice and I think it made her happy not to have to put covers on the couch and chairs to hide the wear and rips.

One of the best things was that my dad stopped drinking. I think being sick with hepatitis and almost dying scared him into giving it up—at least for then. Since he was no longer drinking, he stopped running with the ladies and my parents weren't fighting all the time. They really seemed happy. Another benefit of him not drinking was he was home more. He and my mother did more together, like go to the movies or a live show. They used to go to a place in South Boston called Blinstrub's Village that had live shows. They saw Milton Berle there once. I guess he actually took a cigarette out of my mother's pack that was on the table. My folks thought it was a hoot. They also took my grandmother to see cabaret singer Ruth Wallace there one time. It was one of my father's favorite places to go and he could afford to do more since he was not drinking his money away.

I loved the pleasant walk to school. There were no more fights to worry about, which was great, and the road was lined with beautiful trees on both sides. Since I spent most of my life until that point in the projects, I was not around trees much and never realized how magnificent they were. I was discovering for the first time how much I really liked them. I felt awe-struck and was surprised to see there were no two trees exactly the same. They were not like the pictures of matching trees I saw in children's books. The beauty of one tree is breathtaking to me. From the many shades of green in springtime to the Technicolor leaves of fall, I am mesmerized by one of God's greatest creations. I always feel a sense of peace and wonder when I gaze at a tree.

My sister Karen went to the Junior High, so I was the oldest now and had to look out for the younger kids. I would walk to school with Linda, Stephen, and Ricky. On the way home we usually walked home with my cousins Bobby, Larry, and Donna. I loved walking with them. They made me laugh all the time. Larry had some funny thing he would do, like pretending he was answering the telephone. I thought it was hysterical and Bobby would laugh like crazy and all his laughing would crack me up. I loved being around him. Anytime I think about Bobby, I swear I can still hear his laughter.

Living there was good for my sister Karen, too. She had a lot of friends and went to all of their birthday parties. When she turned fourteen, my mother gave her a birthday party and invited all her friends, but would not let any of us kids attend. I still remember how angry I was. I literally thought my mother was a bitch because she put us kids in one of the bedrooms to watch TV. I thought it was a very mean thing for my mother to do to us.

I managed to sneak out of the bedroom for a few minutes while everybody was dancing and having a good time. There was all kinds of food — sandwiches, chips cookies, cake, ice cream, and soda. I had never seen anything like it. And it was so weird seeing my parents dance. Of course I got caught and sent back into the bedroom with the other kids. It didn't make sense to me that just because we were younger we were not allowed to go. I've never understood how or why my mother did that to us. It was the first birthday party in our house. She tried to make me feel better by saying I would have one when I turned fourteen, that we all would, but it would never come to pass. My uneventful twelfth birthday came and went a month later.

All of us kids had more freedom living there. When we moved in, Karen was thirteen, I was eleven, and Linda was ten. That summer, for a nickel each, we three would take the train, then a bus, to the public pool in Brighton. We always asked the bus driver for a transfer, which we used for bus ride home, but we paid both ways for the train. It cost only fifteen cents to use the pool for the day. We almost always ran into our old neighbors from 940 Parker Street and it was fun when we did.

They had lifeguards at the pool and thank God for that. Karen talked me into jumping into the ten-foot side of the pool one day, telling me to do the dog paddle and I would be fine. I jumped and she didn't think, jumped right after me, and almost landed on me. That scared me so bad I started sinking and was grabbing her pushing her under trying to stay on top of the water. The lifeguard jumped in and scooped us both up in one arm. I was crying and thanking him for saving me. He scolded me and told me not to come to the deep side again, and I never did.

I always loved swimming, so not long after that happened, I

decided I needed to learn to swim and would walk to a place called Curtis Hall to take swimming lessons. Monday, Wednesday, and Friday was girls day and it only cost a nickel. I was glad it was not far from where I lived. The swimming test was not hard. I just had to swim back and forth across the five-foot-deep area a couple of times. I was scared, because five feet was way over my head, but I passed the test and felt like a million bucks. There was nobody to tell about it, but it was a personal accomplishment for me.

I didn't have many friends, but was pretty happy for the most part because I had so much to do. Besides going to Curtis Hall, I would go up the street from where my aunt Ester lived to see the horses. There was a small riding school there and I would watch them ride each Thursday night. I wanted to take riding lessons, but never asked because I knew my parents could not afford it. I used to imagine I was learning to ride and listened to everything I could hear the instructor tell them. I remember watching them post while riding. It looked pretty easy and I was sure I would be able to do that.

I was no longer able to visit Aunt Joan because she lived too far away for me to walk, but I started visiting my aunt Ester, who only lived one street over. I loved going there as much as I had Aunt Joan's. She would always talk to me and take the time to listen to me. Sometimes when I was there, Uncle Bob would bring his guitar out. I think he was learning to play. When he would sit down and start to play, my cousins would join him and they would all sing together. He always invited me to join them, which I did. My father always told me not to sing; that I was tone deaf. So at first I was afraid to sing with them. But since my uncle never said anything and always encouraged me to sing, I got over my fear and sang my heart out. I still remember him singing the song *Tom Dooley*, a sad song about a guy who killed someone and was going to be hanged. I thought it must be one of his favorite songs because he always played it. He never knew those sing-alongs with him and my cousins meant the world to me.

Aunt Ester and Uncle Bob were the best. It was fun living

near them. Until we moved there, I barely knew them, having seen them only a handful of times. Now I was spending as much time with them as I could. As I said earlier, I gravitate toward nice people and *they were the best!*

My uncle had a turquoise and white boat. In the summertime, he would take the family to the lake almost every day. He owned a window washing business so he could make his own hours. On the best sunny days, he would get out of work early, usually right after school was out.

I always walked home from school with my cousins. Sometimes, he would tell me to ask my mother if I could go to the lake with them. She always said yes to that. I would grab my swimsuit and off I would run to my aunt's house. I didn't always get to go, but I lived for those days I did. I didn't want to be rude, so I never once asked if I could go with them, but I prayed all the time they would ask me. I loved being with my aunt, uncle, and cousins. It didn't matter if they were going on the boat or not. I always wanted to be with them. Looking back, me being there so much was probably a pain in the neck, but they never said anything about it. Perhaps they knew about my own family dynamics.

Uncle Bob was an extraordinary water-skier. He had all kinds of skies—regular, slalom, and trick skis. He could even ski backwards! My aunt and all the kids skied as well. My aunt, uncle, and Bobby all took turns slalom skiing. That summer, Uncle Bob was teaching Bobby to ski backwards. I loved watching them and thought they were all amazing. I believe that summer was cousin Donna's first year on skis. She was five. I think Larry skied at times, too, but I don't remember it being a big thing for him. After a day at the lake, just as the sun was setting, we would sometimes get ice cream. I enjoyed orange sherbet for the first time when I was with them.

Late one summer afternoon, my uncle asked me if I would like to learn to water ski. I could hardly believe it. Of course I did, but I would never ask to go to the lake with them, nor would I have asked to try skiing. Again, I didn't want to be rude, but boy-oh-boy did I want to. It was beyond my wildest dreams!

He told me I had to prove I could swim. He said he was going to throw me off the boat going 30 mph, and I would have let him, but I was glad he was just kidding about throwing me off. But he did want to make sure I could swim. I told him I just passed the swimming test at Curtis Hall so he told me to jump into the lake.

The thought of the lake being so deep scared me. I previously only swam in a five-foot-deep pool and didn't realize water is water, so I was scared when I started to sink. My uncle jumped in to help me and I almost drowned us both by pushing him under the water. My aunt threw a boat cushion into the water and I grabbed onto it. Then Uncle Bob pulled the cushion and me to the boat. I still remember how horrible I felt about almost drowning us.

Age 11

He never made me feel bad about that day. He simply asked me what happened and I told him when I thought about how deep it was I got scared since I only swam in five feet water. He explained it doesn't matter how deep the water is that you swim in, it's the same. I later heard him say something to my aunt about learning a lesson about never jumping in when someone is afraid like that; that he should have thrown the cushion first.

I was shocked when he asked if I was ready to learn to ski. I couldn't believe he was still going to teach me after I had almost drowned him, but I was ready to learn. He told Bobby to get me his life jacket and skis. Then he set the boat up with two ski lines. I saw that many times before when he skied with Bobby.

He told me how to bend my knees and straighten as the boat pulled me up. I was so excited. The boat went forward and so did I. I got up my first time trying. I think everybody but me was shocked. I knew I could do it. I had been watching and paying attention all summer. I didn't go a great distance but I went far enough. I was able to get right back up on them even in deep water. I was a natural. My uncle could not believe I learned that quick. It was the best summer of my life.

My aunt and uncle were the most awesome people I knew. They seemed to like me, and I adored them. I never felt uncomfortable around them or felt like I could not be myself at their house. When we sang, I was not afraid of getting laughed at. Looking back, I was a lucky girl to have two aunts and uncles I loved who I knew cared about me. I know my aunts would tell my mother how good I was when I was with them and I knew they said they didn't understand why she felt like I was so hard.

I had other aunts I loved who loved me, like my dad's sister Barbara, but I didn't get to see her often. When I did, I always had a good time at her house. She had the best coloring books and the biggest box of crayons. My favorite coloring book in the world was Sleeping Beauty and she had it. She also made pudding cake for me, which I loved.

One of the best things about our move to Rossmore Road was my mother was no longer angry all the time. It was *so* nice. We still occasionally had our days, but for the most part, we got along much better while we lived there. She was so much happier, too, and spent a lot time with her sister Ester doing stuff like shopping. My younger sister Paula was five as was my cousin Donna. They were in the same class for kindergarten, so my aunt and mother would walk the girls to school each day and hang out until the kids came home.

Mom said living on Rossmore Road was a special time for her. It gave her time to connect with her sister, who she adored. Since they did not grow up together, there were many years they hardly saw each other. Mom felt like Aunt Ester was pretty much the only family she had now. Her aunts didn't like my dad, so my mother stayed away from them. Her father was an alcoholic who was still drinking, so other than him coming to our house for Sunday dinner, she never saw him.

It wasn't until years later, when I was an adult, that my mother told me about getting to know her sister during the year we lived on Rossmore Road. She told me how precious the time they spent together was for her. I finally understood why, when I used to beg her to let me go with them, she always said no. As a child, I just thought she didn't want me around, but it had nothing to do with me. She just wanted time for herself with her sister.

Though I was only eleven years old, I was allowed to babysit. I liked kids and was pretty good with them. There was a family across the street from my aunt, the Joneses, who had three kids. I babysat for them during the week for about an hour a day, from five o'clock to six or a little after. Their mother worked down the street at the Forrest Hills Factory Outlet and she had to be at work before her husband got home. On Sunday nights the whole family would visit the mother's sister in Danvers and they let me go with them so I could keep an eye on the kids while they visited. We always came home late at night. They would drop me off in front of my house. I never told them, or anyone, that to get in the house, I had to climb up the back porch steps and then over the railing to get in my brother's third-floor bedroom window. I guess I felt ashamed that my mother locked me out. She knew climbing in the window was the only way I had to get in. If there were no lights on in the yard, it was hard to see, and some nights, I was afraid of falling. I felt sad she locked me out and didn't understand why she locked the door when she knew I was not home. Of course, I never questioned her about it back then, but it was a question I asked her when I was an adult. She just said, "I knew you could climb in the window with no problem."

The window was not as easy to open as my mother thought it was. I had to lean way over the porch to pry it. Then I had to stretch my left leg over the porch and into the window. And it hurt my feelings that she didn't seem to care enough about me to leave the door unlocked. I babysat for that family for a long time.

That winter the Joneses moved to Malden, a city about five miles north of Boston. I was allowed to go to babysit on weekends. I would take a train, then a bus on Saturday, spend the night, and head home Sunday afternoon. I loved going there and spending the time with Mrs. Jones until one morning I woke up and her husband was lying on top of me. I was afraid and had a sick feeling in my stomach. I was so scared I closed my eyes, but I think he knew I was awake because he left. I peeked at him as he walked away. He had on powder blue pajama bottoms and a white t-shirt. I felt sick inside and I didn't know what to think.

Later, when he was not in the house, I told his wife what happened. She had this idea about looking in the hamper to see if the pajamas were in it. I was not sure what that would mean, but she said, "Okay. Let's look in the hamper to see if the pajamas are there." They were in it, but not right on top. They were under a few t-shirts. She said, "See it is not true or they would have been on top." She then sat me down and said she understood why I thought that. Then she explained to me why I thought something like that happened. She said it was because I must have wanted it to happen, so I imagined it. I tried telling her I was sure of what happened and that I didn't imagine it. In my heart, I knew what happened. It was exactly what I told her. But she insisted that it was my imagination. She told me it was my imagination so many times I began to think maybe she was right. I left later that day and never went back.

I didn't tell anyone else about what happened for fear they would say the same thing she said. The thought that I dreamed that up made me feel awful, guilty, and ashamed of myself, even though I didn't understand it. I was only eleven years old and didn't know about sex yet. I still thought they cut babies out of bellies. I began to think I must be a bad person to dream that up. I also thought I must be crazy. I eventually forgot about it for many years, although the memory would one day resurface when I was an adult and I would feel the full reality of it and the damage it did to me. I suffered an immense amount of shame about that morning and what I was made to believe about it.

* * *

Our move put us in a new parish, but we continued to attend church and, for us kids, Sunday School. That spring, I turned twelve and attended special catechism classes. It was time for me to make my Confirmation. Apparently during the ceremony, we had to kiss the Cardinal's ring. It is safe to say I was rebellious and planned to make believe. I was not going to kiss anybody's ring, even if he was a Cardinal. I was not sure my pretending would count with God, but I sure hoped it would. My birthday was just weeks before the ceremony that was held one afternoon after school. I was so excited walking to church with my mother, dressed in the pink suit and white pumps I got for Easter that year. When we reached the church, my mother went inside while I went to my classroom to put on the red catechism robe and cap. They were like the ones students wear when they graduate high school or college. I remember lining up and walking down the aisle with my group. Just as with my First Communion, my mother's family was all there watching me.

It was very special being Confirmed in this Church because it was the parish in which my mother grew up. Her parents grew up in it as well. Saint Thomas Aquinas Church in Jamaica Plain, Massachusetts is where my mother was baptized and made her First Holy Communion, and Confirmation. Both my mother's parents also received all the sacraments here including the Sacrament of Marriage. Being Confirmed here made me a part of my mother's family legacy within this Church. That made this day extra special for me. I thought about my mother's mother and, although I never met her, I believed she was smiling down on me that day.

* * *

Spring was beautiful that year and I was looking forward to summer with great anticipation. I was hoping I would get to water-ski again. Although summer had not officially begun, on the days that were warm enough, my uncle was back at the lake as often as the weather permitted. Sometimes I was able to go with them. He skied with a wet suit until the water was warm enough to ski without one, which was when my cousins and I started skiing again. My uncle allowed me to cross the wake, which was scary at first, but a lot of fun. I loved skiing and loved that my uncle gave me the chance to do it. No longer having to stay directly behind the boat, and crossing the wake made me feel like a big shot. I could cross the right wake with ease but the left wake was a different story. I fell a lot before I got that one mastered.

That summer, my parents decided we were going to take a vacation. We never before went on a vacation. We were going to visit my grandmother in New Hampshire for a week as soon as school was out. My dad bought camping stuff so we could camp out in my grandmother's back yard. Early on the morning of June 25, 1966, my father packed up the car and we headed for New Hampshire. I always remembered that date because the night before we left, he took us to Revere Beach Amusement park and let us ride all the rides we wanted. It was huge and such a fun night. My dad took us to carnivals before, small ones in church parking lots, but this was a biggie, the biggest in eastern Massachusetts, and I had never been there. I wanted to ride the roller coaster, but my mother wouldn't let me.

I really didn't want to go to New Hampshire the next day. I wanted to stay here and hang out with my friend Vicky. She was moving in a week and I would not be back before she left. I also wanted to be able to go to the lake with my aunt and uncle afternoons when he got out of work.

We went to New Hampshire, but didn't end up camping in my grandmother's yard. We camped at a campground not far from her house. I was having so much fun swimming every day it didn't take me long to forget I didn't want to come. For the most part, I was alone at the campsite as well as at the pool they had.

I wondered where Karen and Linda went mornings before I woke up or to where they took off while I was in the shower. Karen didn't want me to hang around her and her friends but let Linda go with her, but I would usually run into her at the recreation center in the afternoon. There she had no choice since she could not make me leave.

There was a record player, and everyone was always dancing. I got along with the other kids, especially those who knew line dances and taught them to us. I loved the dance we did to the song *Last Kiss*. I think it was called *The Snake*. I never really danced before that and I loved it. I especially loved to line dance since it made me feel part of the group, which was a whole new experience for me and was where my love of line dancing as an adult came from.

I wanted to be able to do the Cha Cha so much, but I had a hard time learning it. Finally Karen said she would teach me. Every afternoon she put on Frankie Valli & The Four Seasons' *Sherry Baby*. Then she would show me the steps again and again until I mastered it. I remember how much fun I had learning it. I was not a quick study, but my sister was patient. I loved to watch Karen dance; she was amazing and knew all the newest dances. Dancing became one of my favorite things, and by watching Karen, I got to be pretty good at it. So much so, I won the big dance contest in eighth grade while Karen won the Senior Dance contest in high school. She was the best dancer in the school.

We were supposed to be at the campground for only one week, but it turned into the entire summer. I wanted to go home. I missed home and my aunt, uncle, and cousins and was glad when summer was over. What I didn't know was I was never going home to Boston again.

Six

My dad decided we would move to New Hampshire. He felt the country was a better place for us to live. I think he decided and told my mother after seeing us so happy all summer and didn't have the heart to bring us back to the City. He was still sober at that time. He got a job in the area and found an apartment. Everyone but me knew we were staying here. My parents left us with my grandmother one Saturday, drove to Jamaica Plain to get our belongings, and moved us into a ranch style duplex in Rochester. It was a very quiet neighborhood with not much to do. The only good thing was it was only a few miles from my grandmother's house.

Still, I was devastated. I loved living on Rossmore Road. I was happy there. I was also mad that everyone but me knew what my parents were doing. How could they do that to me? How could they not tell me or let me say good-bye to my friends and family in Boston? I was sure I would never see them again and cried for days. It felt like more of the mean stuff my mother did, which made me hate her more than I already did, if that was even possible. She never cared how I felt, ever, and I hated to be stuck in this family.

I despised the new place. There were no girls my age in the neighborhood, just boys of all ages, and I hated boys. There was one I met as soon as we moved there who I especially hated. His name was Rusty. He was fourteen and I was twelve.

He told me he liked me and wanted me to be his girlfriend. He would follow me around on his bike all the time, but I was not into boys. What I was into was catching tree toads, building houses with bamboo for them to live in, and digging pools for them to swim in using foil stolen from the kitchen when my mother was not looking. I also liked playing army soldiers with my brothers since I could be the general, roller-skating, riding bikes when I could borrow one, and swimming. I still loved swimming. And I was certainly *not* going to be his, or anyone's girlfriend.

* * *

I was not a girly girl by any stretch of the imagination. I was the complete opposite, a tom boy and a tough kid. I had lived my whole life in the city of Boston. I was a scrapper who could kick the crap out of most boys my age and was never afraid of them, even though they were often bigger than me. But it was different with Rusty. Him I was afraid of. He was not an average fourteen-year-old. He was much bigger than other boys his age and I was still smaller than the girls my age. I didn't ever want to get into a fight with him. I was glad he liked me, even though I didn't want to be his girlfriend. But my fear of boys was well placed. Rusty would make me despise them and him.

* * *

Not long after we moved to Rochester, my father began drinking again and was back to running around. My mother was broken-hearted about it and it didn't take long until she was completely obsessed again. She was angrier than I ever saw her. I believe having a year and a half of my dad not drinking, and things being so good, caused her to resent his drinking more than ever. It was not long until she was back to the painful place in which she spent most of her marriage. Looking back, I see how my dad's return to drinking brought my mother to a new low. It seemed to happen overnight, like a bad dream, like nothing had changed. I think it left mom with a civilian kind of shell shock. She was madder and more hurt than I ever remembered her being in the past, and her relationship with me went from bad to worse. In the past, she would say mean stuff to me to break my heart and make me cry, or punish me by making me go in my room. Now she was losing control with me, like she could hardly stop when she put her hands on me.

I stayed away from her as much as possible and did my best not to upset her because if she got her hands on me it was always more than a slap. She was so mad all the time, and so easily set off, I was afraid of her

One time, a friend from Boston let her daughter come to visit. She went into my mothers' room and got into her makeup. I got mad at her, put her suitcase on the front porch, and said she should go home. I know it wasn't nice of me, but I was so mad that she got into my mother's makeup I could not help myself. I would have been killed for doing something like that. My mother was not home at the time. When she did come home and learned what happened, she was really mad at me. She came into my bedroom and was yelling at me when she took off her high heels and started hitting me with one. Both my calves were bleeding where the heel had pierced them. When she stopped hitting me, she told me to get out and not let anyone see my legs or tell anyone what she did.

I couldn't get out of there fast enough. I ran down to the river to cry. Rusty saw me heading for the river and followed. I had shorts on so he saw my legs bleeding and asked me what happened. Even though my mother told me not to tell anyone I told him that my mother beat me with her high heel. Then I told him to leave me alone. He left, and I climbed a tree and stayed in it for hours, just crying.

I spent a lot of time in that tree by the river. It was my favorite hiding place, so high nobody ever looked for me there. It was the place I would go when I was hurting. I would sit in the tree for hours, just thinking.

In order to climb it, I had to climb a thing we called the catwalk. The catwalk was a platform roughly fifteen feet high, ten feet long, and three feet wide. We kids used it to swing over the river on a rope and jump in. The grownups said it was dangerous, but I didn't think so. I loved swinging back and forth over the river. If I was the only one there, which was rare, I would swing back and forth for a long time before I jumped. Rusty and some of the other kids were afraid to do it, but not me. I was not afraid of much.

Looking back, I can see how dangerous it was swinging out from the catwalk, but I didn't know it back then. If I had ever fallen, it would have killed me. Sometimes my friend from roller-skating would come to the river with her older brother to hang out with me and swim. We would sit on the catwalk and watch as he and the other boys jumped from a tree on the other side into the river. Now *that* looked scary to me, but I might have tried it if I was tall enough to reach a tree limb to climb up to jump. Those boys were a lot older than us, so we stayed on our side of the river while they were there. Sometimes when they were gone, my friend and I would swim across the river and jump off the dock.

* * *

It was not long after we moved to Rochester that summer ended and school began. I was glad to see summer end. I was going into seventh grade. Though I was a little apprehensive about going to a new school, I was not terrified. I changed schools so many times since the third grade I was used to it. I was not a shy kid and never had trouble meeting people. Though I never had lots of friends, I usually had at least a couple. There were things about going to school in New Hampshire that were nice. One was the school bus. I loved that. Not that I minded walking, but it was nice not having to walk when the weather was bad. Also, they had hot lunches. I loved that, too. No more cheese sandwiches ever!

I met Ann in school and we became best friends. We both loved roller-skating and went every Saturday night, sometimes Friday, and occasionally Sunday, too. And I was sometimes allowed to spend the night at her house. Ann and I would ride the school bus to her house after school on Friday and go roller-skating on Saturday. I would meet my sisters there and walk home with them.

Ann had an older sister who was getting married, and a brother who was fifteen. Her brother had a guitar and played the song *Winchester Cathedral* over and over, which reminded me of Uncle Bob playing Tom Dooley. I would lie in bed listening to him play and be lulled to sleep. I loved spending the night at Ann's house. There was never any fighting there.

I once spent the whole weekend at Ann's. My mother told me I was not allowed to go skating on Saturday and to make sure Ann's family knew that. I don't remember why I couldn't go. I told Ann about not being allowed skating, and she said it was fine, we could hang out at her house, but when Saturday night arrived, she talked me into going. I knew that it was not a good idea, but she insisted my mother would never know, so I went, and was skating around when I saw my mother come into the rink. I started shaking and skated as fast as I could to the girl's bathroom. I pulled the skates off and asked someone to please bring them to the desk after I left. I was terrified, praying my mother did not see me on the skates. I thought if I convinced her I was just there but not skating she might go easy on me. No such luck. She saw me on the skates. When I reached her she started slapping me in front of the whole place. I was so embarrassed I felt like I would die. A lump formed in my throat and I had to choke back the tears. It was not from her hitting me. I was used to that. It was from the shame I felt that she lost it in front of everybody.

The slapping continued all the way home. Thank God we didn't live far. Rusty's mother drove mine to see if I was there and I believe she regretted it as she kept telling my mother she should stop hitting me. When we reached home my mother yelled at me to get in my room. I ran as fast as I could and didn't come out until I knew everyone was asleep, and then only to use the bathroom and brush my teeth. I can tell you this—I learned my lesson. I would never again sneak someplace my mother told me not to go.

I knew I deserved to be in trouble for sneaking roller-skating, but to do what she did was wrong. I knew it was not right for her to hit me the way she did but there was nothing I could do about it

I wondered how I was going to show my face to anyone. I hoped they would forget since I knew it would be a while before I would be allowed to go roller-skating again. I was not sure how long it would take for my mother to get over being mad at me, but I was not about to mention skating, no matter how long I had to wait. Eventually she said I could go with my sisters one night. I don't know what prompted her decision but I didn't ask. I was too afraid she might start slapping me again.

I really tried to be good, and for the most part, I was. But like every kid, I wasn't perfect. I knew I shouldn't have gone skating, but my friend kept insisting and I let her convince me, thinking I'd get away with it. Boy did I calculate that wrong and the price I paid was high. I was embarrassed when people asked if I was ok. I hated they knew my mother hit me. Most of my friends' mothers never hit them and I could tell they felt sorry for me. I hated that most of all, so I told them it was my fault and I deserved it for not listening. Eventually it seemed forgotten.

* * *

I had the best Christmas of my life that year. I was not a kid who ever said I wanted this or that for Christmas. I was all too aware of how little money my parents had, so I never wanted to tell them I wanted any certain thing. With six of us, I never wanted to put them in a spot to feel like they had to give me something they might not be able to afford, but that Christmas was different. When my mother asked me what I wanted, I didn't hesitate. I wanted roller skates and didn't care if it was the only thing I got. They were the only thing I wanted, but never thought I would get them. Then the last boxes came out from under the tree, and they were skate cases with new roller skates inside them for me, Karen, and Linda. I was the happiest kid in the world that morning. I felt like I had arrived. I had my own skates which would save me fifty cents rental fee each night. I also had a case to put them in like some of the other kids who went skating. I was truly in heaven that day and got to go roller-skating that night. It's a little embarrassing to say I felt like a king walking into the roller rink with my shiny new bright red and white skate case with my very own roller skates, but that's how it was. It was special because many kids did not have their own skates and case. It was an amazing feeling. I tired of the case quickly though. It was heavy, and carrying it back and forth the mile and a quarter to the rink was a pain. I soon decided it was much easier to just tie my skates together and throw them over my shoulder, and I was all for easy.

Rochester was turning out to be a pretty good place for me. I had roller-skating each weekend and that was enough for me. Then there was a thing the cool kids did roller-skating. It was called the Sunset Bounce, named after the roller rink. It's hard to explain how they did it. They had a way of dragging their right skate across the floor as they rounded a corner and it bounced to the music. It was the coolest thing to see. When couples were skating, they were in sync and they looked awesome. I loved watching them and wanted to learn it so bad. I practiced all the time until I was good at it. I wanted to be cool like the older kids, but just about the time I mastered it, my roller-skating days came to an abrupt end.

We were getting ready to move again.

Why can't we just stay put? I thought. Every time things were good, we would move. This was going to be the fifth move since I was in third grade. Most of the moves took place early in the summer but this one was happening in the middle of this school year.

I was in the seventh grade and already struggling with English. I was failing all the tests, so they made me stay after school for an entire week to get extra help. The last school bus to East Rochester left later than all the other busses and I got permission from the school to take that bus every day for a week. It dropped me off in front of my grandmother's house. She left the door unlocked for me. When she came home from work, she would cook us something to eat, then drive me home. That was a great week for me, even though I had to stay after school. With the extra help I got, I was able to pass the retest, so I didn't have to stay after school anymore.

I felt a bit sad going straight home again because I loved going to my grandmother's house, partly because she was a great cook but mostly because she loved me, and I adored her. I loved the time we spent together that week. I knew when we moved, I would not see my her much since I would have no way to get to her house. At least here I could ride a bike to go to see her on the weekends. I loved riding bikes although I didn't own one. One of the neighborhood boys would let me use his bike sometime. It was a black stingray with a banana seat. It was the newest trend in bikes and was very cool, so, I would borrow his bike and ride to my grandmother's house some Saturdays. Sometimes my sister would say she could not believe I would want to ride that far, but I never minded the three miles each way. It didn't seem far to me, but as I said, I loved to ride. It was fun, not work.

Seven

Our new home was in Dover, New Hampshire. Though it was only about fifteen miles from Rochester, it might just as well have been a million miles. I knew my roller-skating days were over. I would have no way to get to the roller rink and there was no roller rink in Dover. I was heartbroken knowing I would not be able to roller-skate or ride to see my grandmother.

My mother got a job at a taxi company as a dispatcher and needed to be closer to work. Also, her friend was moving there as well, which meant Rusty would be living in Dover, too. I was still afraid of him, though I can't say exactly why. He followed me on his bike all the time, which I hated, and I just felt afraid of him, like I sensed something. It might have been his size that scared me. He was so much bigger than me and my instinct told me not to trust him alone. I didn't like how he looked at me and made sure I was never alone with him. I hated that he was moving to the same area we were, and only a few streets from our new house.

Things at home were getting worse for all of us. My mother worked nights, which meant Karen was in charge again. Other than occasional babysitting, she had not been in charge for almost two years. Now she was turning fifteen and would be babysitting every night of the week while my mother worked. My mother left for work at three-thirty, right after we got home from school, and didn't get home until after midnight during the week and two o'clock on weekends. She worked six nights a week and her day off was always a weeknight but, a different one each week.

* * *

I turned thirteen forty-five days after my sister turned fifteen. It was the middle of the school year and I hated my new school. It was not like the other school, which was a Junior High, just seventh and eighth grades. This new school was first through eight. We didn't change classes; we were with the same teacher and same kids all day long. I was starting to develop and the boys in the class were teasing me. One boy I called Creep the Greek to my girlfriends. I sat right in front of him and would notice him staring at me if I had to get up in class.

One day, he tapped me on the shoulder. When I turned around, he asked me where I got the oranges. I had no idea what he was talking about. Then he motioned on his chest and said, "These oranges." The boys around him heard it all and started laughing. I felt like I could die. I didn't want to have breasts. I wanted to slap his face for saying that but knew I would get in trouble for it so I didn't. I never turned around again when he tapped my shoulder.

I didn't pass that year and had to stay back, which was so humiliating. It was the last day of school when I found out. The town had built a new high school and turned the old high school into a Junior High with just seventh and eighth grades. I figured the kids in my class might not realize I was not in the eighth grade until eight grade graduation, and by then maybe they would have forgotten about me. But school was out for now, and I was glad it was summer.

I learned there was a school bus that took kids to a place called Bellamy three times a week during the summer for swimming. It was the Bellamy River. I still loved swimming and looked forward to it. The bus brought us down and back Monday, Wednesday, and Friday. My mother would fix us lunches and all my siblings went most of the time. I was in heaven swimming again.

I met a girl named Sally, and we became friends. She would be in the seventh grade, too. She lived about three miles from my house. On the days we didn't go to Bellamy, I would walk to her house spend the day, and then walk home. Sally, her sister Jackie, and I would listen to music and make up dance routines. Our favorite song at the time was *These Boots Are Made for Walking* by Nancy Sinatra. Sally had a big family and we loved putting on shows for them. Her mother was so nice. Sally and her sister came to my house once that summer. My aunt said she would pierce everybody's ears and they got permission from their mom and came over. Sally changed her mind when she saw how it was done. We put ice on our ears to numb them then my aunt would put a needle through our ear lobe. Sally decided to let her mother buy her some sleepers after watching that, but her sister got her ears pierced that day with the rest of us. For the most part, that summer was turning out pretty good. I spent days visiting Sally. Nights I would hang out with the kids in the neighborhood and play kick the can and hide and seek. That all changed on July fourth.

The Fourth of July was a painful day for me. I was supposed to go to a friend's house and go to the fireworks with the family. That didn't happen because about two weeks before the Fourth, one of the boys in the family needed a sleeping bag to go on a Boy Scout trip. We had sleeping bags so I called my mother at work one night and asked if he could borrow one. Right away she said yes. He came to the house to get it early that Saturday morning. My parents were still sleeping. I woke my mother up and told her Dave was here to get the sleeping bag. My mother told me to take the camper key out of my father's pants pocket on the dresser, give Dave the sleeping bag, and put the key back. Though I'd never before taken anything out of my dad's pocket, I did what my mother said to do.

On the Fourth of July, Dad went into the camper for something and noticed a sleeping bag gone. Since they were stacked on the table it was easy to see because there were three stacks of two and then one. My dad was not happy since he knew he was the only one with a key to get in there. He asked my mother about the sleeping bag. What she apparently said was, "Ask your daughter Patty." He asked me if I knew where the sleeping bag was. I told him I lent it to Dave for a Boy Scout camping trip. He lost it and screamed at me for going in his pants pocket and taking the key. I was crying and saying, "But dad…" but he would not listen. He just yelled at me not to "but dad" him. He sent me to my room, came in, and took off his belt. He never before hit me with a belt. In fact, I had not even been spanked by him since I was eight. Then he told me to lie on my stomach across my bed and he hit me with the belt four or five times. I didn't cry, but I was in shock at what was happening to me. I don't remember it hurting. I only remember I felt rage inside for the first time in my life. It would not be the last. It was a feeling I would become accustomed to.

My father told me before he left the room I was staying in my room until tomorrow, and I was not going to the fireworks with my friends like I planned. He said he bought a watermelon, my favorite, and I would not have any of that either. I was not allowed to come down for dinner that night as well. I spent the rest of the evening listening to the other kids downstairs laughing and having fun as rage welled up inside me. It was a feeling I never before had and could not wait to get my hands on my mother. Or I should say mouth. I wanted to ask her how she could do such a thing to me; lie to my father about the sleeping bag and act like Miss Innocent when she gave me permission. She was in the room when I took the key at her direction and put it back. Knowing the truth, I didn't understand how she could let me get hit and punished. I was so angry I don't think I slept at all that night.

This began a new chapter in my life, one where I learned I could never trust either of my parents. I always knew Mother didn't care about me and that her behavior was bad with me, but I would never have dreamed she would stoop so low as to let my father think I just went into his pants pocket without permission. I felt completely betrayed by her. I learned that day she now had the power to get me in trouble with my dad. It was an all-time low for me. I hated him as much as her because he wouldn't even listen to my side of the story. He shut me down every time I tried to explain, leaving me completely defenseless. Even today, when I feel similarly shut down, it creates the same sense of rage I felt that day.

My father came to my room in the morning to tell me I was grounded in the house but could come out of my room. He also told me I was not to say one word about the whole incident. I was still trying to get him to listen to the truth about what happened, but he told me to shut up, it was over. I shut up to him, but it was not over as far as I was concerned. I was not planning to shut up. I had every intention to talk to my mother about it. I wanted her to tell me how she could do that to me. I wanted to make her tell my dad the truth. My rage was so strong I didn't know what else to do. It was as if it compelled me to say something to her. I was too angry to feel fear of her at that time. I knew she might slap me, but she could not physically harm me since my dad was still home. I knew he would not let her kill me. He would send me back to my room if he found out and maybe hit me with the belt again, but I didn't care anymore what either of them did. I was willing to risk whatever happened to try to get her to tell him the truth.

Since I didn't get supper the night before, I was starving, and went into the kitchen to get some cereal. My mother was peeling potatoes. I leered at her and whispered, "Tell him the truth."

Her answer was, "Didn't your father tell you not to talk about it?"

I was so angry I asked, "When are you going to tell him the truth? How could you lie?"

At that point, she said just loud enough for my dad to hear, "Didn't your father tell you not to talk about it."

My father heard her and bellowed from the other room "Patsy! Didn't I tell you to not talk about that? Get back in your room for the rest of the day."

I would spend the next few days in my room. I could not

stop demanding she tell my dad the truth until I was too tired of being shut up in my room all the time. I felt such betrayal by my mother letting me get in trouble for something I had permission to do. I lost all hope and trust in both my parents from that moment on. As far as I was concerned, they could both go straight to hell. That was how I felt. I knew then I was alone in this world. I always trusted that my dad believed in me but now, he didn't even listen. She managed to take away even that. She won, and that was even more painful than her lie.

* * *

When I was finally allowed to go out, I spent the next two weeks swimming with my friends at Bellamy and walking to Sally's to hang out with her and her sister. One day, I had to stay home from Bellamy. I don't remember why, but I didn't get to go. I imagine I was in trouble for something. My sisters and brothers were gone, and my mother left. She told me not to let anybody in the house.

Rusty and another boy, the brother of Dave to whom I lent the sleeping bag, came to the back door. They said they wanted me to let them in to get a drink of water. It was the last week of July and real hot outside. I told them I was not allowed to let anybody in the house. So, they asked me if they could come in the cellar and get one. Since it technically was not in the house, I thought it would be ok to let them in there. We had a sink in the cellar, so I brought down two glasses for them to use. Letting them in was a decision I would regret the rest of my life.

I would never have opened the door for just Rusty. I was afraid of him enough that I made sure I was never alone with him. I was not afraid of the other boy at all. I could kick his face in and he and I both knew it. These boys were part of a group of us that played kick the can, hide and seek, and softball all the time. We rode the bus to Bellamy together. They were not strangers to me. The other boy who was with Rusty was made fun of a lot because he had crooked teeth. The kids called him that. I didn't call him names. I was not that kind of kid. I didn't like bullying. He was a year younger than me and I was always nice to him. He was not big, just an average twelve-year-old, but he was taller than me. I was still small for my age and probably didn't weigh more than eighty pounds. I know I wore size ten little kids' clothes. Rusty of course was a year older than when we first met. He was fifteen now and he had grown even taller and fatter. I can't stress the difference in our sizes enough. He was huge compared to me.

When I came down the stairs to the cellar Rusty and the other kid were standing by the sink. I handed them the glasses. Rusty got a drink and put the glass down. Then he grabbed me by my wrists and pushed me on the pile of dirty clothes in front of our washing machine. It happened so quick I didn't have time to think. Rusty was kneeling at my head holding both wrists. The other boy was on top of me pulling at my pants. I couldn't hit him because Rusty had my arms pinned to the floor. I didn't know what to do. My head was spinning. I could barely understand what was happening to me. I was in reaction mode. I remember thinking I needed to keep my legs crossed as tight as I could. I was thinking that would stop him from doing what I believed he was planning to do. I didn't know very much about sex and had never heard the word rape. The only thing I knew about sex really was that it was something you did when you were married and I was just barely thirteen years old. My mother was not big about talking to us about such things. I was so scared but had no idea what to do to stop this. I knew I could have kicked the crap out of Crooked Teeth (my new name for him). He knew it too. But I could not fight Rusty he was too big. And I could not fight them both together.

I screamed and yelled but nobody was home. I did everything I could to get away. I even begged Rusty to let go of me, but he did not. I lost the fight. I was now looking down at what was happening to me feeling nothing. Rusty didn't rape me, only held me for the other boy. I hated them both and myself for letting them in the cellar. When they heard noises upstairs as my siblings returned from Bellamy, they ran out the cellar door. That may be the reason Rusty didn't rape me as well.

I didn't know what to do. I was in complete shock. The only feeling I had was one of being completely empty. I pulled my pants up and sat on the pile of dirty laundry for a long time. Nobody came down the cellar. Eventually I made my way out of the house through the cellar door and ran to a girlfriend's house who I knew had cigarettes. She was always trying to get me to smoke, something I never wanted to do. When she answered the door, all I said to her was, "Teach me to smoke." She came out of the house and we went up the street behind the Clam Hut. She gave me a cigarette and taught me how to inhale. I spent the next hour practicing how to inhale. That began an addiction to smoking that would last for many years. I went home and right up the stairs to bed. I didn't say a word to anyone. My mother was at work, which was a huge relief.

I don't remember much about the next few weeks. I was still going to Bellamy and walking to my friend Sally's house. I would like to say I was having fun, but I just felt empty. Every day blended in with the next. There were a few times I felt rage, and the rage was better than the emptiness I felt the rest of the time.

Crooked Teeth had brains enough to stay away from me. I might have killed him if I saw him. But Rusty would taunt me by standing across the street from my house when he saw me outside. That was great for me because I was not afraid of him anymore. I decided he better be afraid of me. Every time I saw him, I would go and punch him as hard as I could in his privates. My being little was good for something. Of course, he would beat the hell out of me, but I didn't care because I knew I hurt him and hurting him was all that mattered to me. I planned to do that every time I saw him.

Our parents were friends. Sometimes, when I would get stuck over his house with my mother, he would come home and I would just leave, making sure to punch him on my way out. Once, I was outside, sitting on the picnic table in the back yard by myself when he came home. He was standing by the back door when I looked up. It had rained that day, so I bent down, picked up a good handful of mud to sling at him. I got about three handfuls thrown before he reached me. I got him good with a mud ball in his face. I was able to get a few punches in before he picked me up and threw me at the house. I was really hurt bad that time. I got the wind knocked out of me and felt like I could not breathe. I limped home and started crying once I was out of his sight. I cried the rest of the way home.

My mother was visiting his mother while the fight was happening. She told me she and his mother could not believe I would continue to start a fight with him knowing he was going to beat me up. Of course she would think that. It would never have occurred to her that maybe I was mad at him for a good reason, even if she didn't know the reason. She knew me better than to think I would start something for nothing. It really hurt me that they watched him throw me against the house and did nothing. I was hurt bad enough that I never hit him again. I just steered clear from that day on. I did however have some satisfaction. Once, when I ended up at his house, I could see some dried mud stuck on cement foundation of the house. It was still there from the day I was slinging it at him. It reminded me that I got a good mud sling at him and I would laugh to myself as I remembered how stupid he looked with mud on his face that day.

Through the years, I have seen TV shows about rape. They always portray the victims as feeling dirty, wanting to shower, not being able to feel clean, but that was not my experience. Perhaps it was because I didn't know boys ejaculated, but I didn't want to take a shower or bath. I didn't want to take my clothes off for any reason. I felt too unsafe to get undressed completely. I would not take off my underpants, and it began causing problems with my mother when she realized I was not bathing, which was not going over well with her. Baths were a daily routine in our house. Prior to the rape, I can't remember a day I did not take a bath or shower. Washing up was not working well, I guess. I never knew how she knew but she knew. She was starting to say things to me like, "You're a little pig." It hurt me so much when she would say that and only added to the hatred for myself I already felt inside.

Sometimes, she would drag me to the bathroom, start running the tub and tell me I was taking a bath. I would pretend to bathe by splashing my hand around so she could hear the water. I did wash up, but did it quick and made sure to wash my hair. I didn't want to be naked. Just the thought of it was unbearable. I had a routine where I changed clothes one piece at a time. I felt safe with my clothes on.

There were times she stood outside the bathroom door and I would actually take a bath. I don't know if it was because I was afraid of getting caught just washing up, or if it was because I felt safe knowing she was there. I so wished I could explain everything to her, but how could I explain what I didn't understand myself.

My fear of being exposed was so great at that time I even slept in my clothes. I don't think anybody knew because I slept on the top bunk. This clothes issue was something I would struggle with at different periods of my life. At times when I felt extremely vulnerable, I would sleep with my clothes on, sure something bad would happen if I didn't.

I eventually did try to tell my mother what Rusty and Crooked Teeth did, but I was so afraid of her, I guess I kind of skirted around it to see how she would take it. I'm not exactly sure what I said, but am sure it was enough that she should have had a good idea what happened. I could see she didn't believe what I was telling her, so I stopped, afraid to push her too far.

Saying I was afraid of her is an understatement. I was terrified of her. She was out of control with me. I never knew what she would do when she was mad. It reached a point with my mother that I could not even trust that I would not get in trouble for stuff I had permission to do. She would allow me to do something, then be mad when I did it.

Eight

Miniskirts were the new fashion, so my mother bought us girls miniskirts. There was a place that just opened for kids to dance, with no drinking allowed, called Midnight Hour, and she promised me I could go. All the kids I knew were going.

I was ready to leave when my mother saw me in the mini skirt and asked me where I thought I was going dressed like that. I reminded her that she bought the skirt for me and said I could go to the Midnight Hour. She just started yelling at me, saying she never said that and I was not going anyplace wearing that skirt. She told me it looked awful on me. She told me Karen and I didn't look good in them because our butts drag on the ground because we were built like her. Of course, me being who I was, I argued with her a little bit. When I told her I thought the skirt looked nice on me even if she didn't think so, she slapped me to the floor, yelling that she hated my guts. When she said that, I started to cry. Even though I always believed she hated me, it was hard hearing her say the words. It tore my heart out.

She said, "There! How do you like it? You tell me you hate me all the time."

I looked her straight in the eye, thinking *that's because I do.* Maybe the look on my face said it because she lost it. She wrapped her hands around my throat and began to choke me. I could not breathe and thought I was going to die as everything was getting black before she let go.

Looking back on some of the stuff that happened to me—not the rape, but other stuff—it was my mouth that got me into trouble. I knew I should not have said, "I think the skirt looks nice on me even if you don't think so." She might not have slapped me if I had stayed quiet, but I just could not stop what I was thinking from rushing out. It was as if there was a slide from my brain to mouth and words would slip right off my tongue.

When she released me, I ran to my room and didn't come out until the next morning. From that moment on, I was more careful when I said stuff to her and made sure I was not close enough for her to reach me. From that day on, if I said anything, especially, "I hate you," I was generally on my way out the door. The words would spill from my mouth as I was running out. It was much safer that way and by the time I got home, she would be gone or have forgotten it.

I learned she was reactionary. Generally, she would not go back to something that happened in the morning unless it was more serious than me saying, "I hate you." We almost always fought in the morning before school.

One day, she was so mad she threw her coffee cup at me. I stepped out of its path and it hit the window and broke the window. My father blamed me for the broken window, saying it was my fault for making my mother throw a cup at me. I knew I would get the blame. According to them, everything was my fault, but I knew it was hers. She didn't have to throw a cup at me.

I was glad it missed me because I could have been really hurt if it hit my head. They never seemed to think about what could happen to me. Sometimes, when they would blame me, I would feel like I would go crazy. Other times I would wonder if I *was* crazy. How could they believe what they were saying? Or was it me that was wrong? I knew some of the stuff I said was wrong, but I was a kid and she was an adult. Wasn't she wrong for throwing a cup? I thought we were both wrong, but they never saw it that way. Sometimes, I would get confused about what happened and would have to think about it over and over to remember it clearly. If I could remember what the truth was, I would know it was not my fault and it would prove to me I was not crazy.

Not wanting to set her off, I did not talk much to my mother. If I did talk to her, I tried to be careful about what I said and how I said it. If I felt she was upset by something I was saying, I would just back off. I think that is what happened when I tried to tell her about Rusty and Crooked Teeth. Many years later we talked about it and she admitted to me that she understood what I was saying but just could not believe something like that really happened. She was in denial about it and I was full of hate and self-loathing about it.

* * *

After what happened with Rusty and Crooked Teeth, one day blended into another. I felt like the walking dead because I had no feelings for a long time, just this emptiness. I don't know how I functioned. I guess I was just on autopilot. Summer was coming to an end soon. School would be starting and I was hopeful I would have something to think about other than what happened that day. Nobody knew but me and them and it was not something I could talk about. I desperately wanted to forget it, but the memory plagued me. Sometimes, when I was at Sally's, I would almost forget about it. She was becoming my best friend in the world. We would be going to the Junior High School together and I hoped she would be in some of my classes, but no such luck.

It was the end of summer, and it was beginning to get dark early now, but I was not always paying attention. I usually left her house by six thirty or so. I had to walk three miles home and wanted to be home before dark. One night I was not watching the time. It was about seven o'clock before I left. I could see it was starting to get dark and was a little uneasy because I had to go by areas that were all woods on one side of the street and on other side were just a few gas stations. This they called the miracle mile. It was secluded and was not a mile

I wanted to walk alone in the dark. And the stretch after that was even more secluded. I hated that I had not paid attention to the time.

As I walked, I noticed a green car pass me, then turn around and pass me again. The car kept turning around and I began to feel afraid because I was almost at the huge section of woods. This was a secluded area but was not the worst yet. When I saw the car go by me the third time I decided I better not stay on this side of the road. I decided I should go to the gas station across the street and ask to use the phone. I was going to call my mother at work. I knew if I told her I was afraid because I was being followed, she would send me a cab. My mother knew me well enough to know I didn't scare easy so she would listen to me. I was shaking as I headed to the gas station. I told the guy that someone was following me that I needed to use the phone to call my mother and that she worked at the taxi company. I could not believe it. That *&#!^$G guy wouldn't let me use the phone! I didn't know what to do. He was the only one there. I started crying, begging him to let me call my mother. I can't tell you how I ended up in a bathroom attached to the station with him, but I did. He didn't rape me but that *$#!ER molested me.

He said he would drive me home. I was afraid, but I let him drive me home thinking at least he was not going to kill me. He talked to me all the way to my house. We lived up the street from a drive-in theater. He kept asking me if I knew what people did in it. I knew all the kids in our neighborhood would sneak in through the woods and sit on blankets and watch the movie for free. I used to do that sometimes with them if there was a good movie showing. He was saying he wanted me to go to the drive-in with him the next night. I was still street smart, so I went along with everything he said. He wanted me to meet him the next night right where he was dropping me off up the street from my house and made sure I knew what time. Then he dropped me off.

I ran home, went to my room, climbed on my bed, and just stared out the window into the dark. I wanted to die. I hated myself for not being able to stop that loser. He was in his late teens or early twenty's I think, not, a grown man like my dad. What a piece of shit he was. I had no intention of meeting him the next night and didn't want to leave my house unless I was with someone. Mostly I just sat in my room looking out the window feeling so very alone. I wish I could say I wanted to tell my mother what happened, but I didn't want to tell anybody. I felt so much shame inside. I believed it was my fault because I could not stop what happened. If I had not been so afraid of the car that was following me, I would have run out of the gas station. That fear kept me trapped. It made me compliant to that person's demand.

I never went to Sally's house again to hang out, but I was able to walk to school with her because we moved just before school started. This was one move I was glad about. I hated where we were because it had too many bad memories, and was glad to be moving closer to town and further away from Rusty and Crooked Teeth.

Sally had to pass by my street, so I would meet her at the corner and continue to school each morning. My street was a long one, about a mile from my house to the corner where I met Sally. Then it was about a mile to school. If I went a different way, it would have cut a mile off my walk, but being able to see my friend was worth the extra mile. We had entirely different classes so, other than the morning walk to school, we didn't see each other anymore.

I no longer had the desire to do anything and pretty much just withdrew for a while. I don't remember doing much other than staring out my bedroom window. Sally and I continued to walk to school until I ended up in reform school. After I went there, we never walked together again. In fact we didn't see each other for thirty-seven years.

* * *

Thinking back, it seems strange we never ran into each other in school, although we were in the same Junior High and High School and hung out in some of the same places. We also both went to the Midnight Hour and Monkey Club as we got older, but never saw each other in either of those places. It was not until we were both close to fifty that I ran into one of her sisters in a gym and asked if she would give Sally my phone number. Although we lost contact for all those years, we had that anchor from the year we were both thirteen and became fast friends again. We look back and laugh about the dance routines we made up, especially to *These Boots Are Made for Walking*. We had a lot of catching up to do. We talked about all the things that were happening in our lives, things we never talked about when we walked to school, like the Midnight Hour and Monkey Club and how young we both got married at seventeen, though neither of us was pregnant. I am so grateful we rekindled our friendship. I can't imagine my life without her in it. It is a blessing I thank God for.

* * *

As Sally and I walked to school that first day, I didn't tell her I was afraid of going. The friend who taught me to smoke was also friends with another girl, Becky, who didn't like me. I met her at Bellamy a few times. She was always trying to start a fight with me. I hated it because she would say stuff like, "Oh look at the tough girl from Boston. I think she thinks she's tough." That kind of stuff. I didn't want to fight her and was able to avoid her throughout the summer, but admit I was afraid of what would happen the first day of school. I knew it would be hard to avoid her. I decided if she was determined to fight me, there was nothing I could do but fight her. I would have to show her I was not afraid of her. Though she was bigger than me, I felt I had the advantage. I was a fighter my whole life up to that point. I could take a beating and keep fighting and never gave up. I always had that going for me. But when I arrived at school that first day, I learned that after she saw me with Cindy and she saw me smoking, she decided she wanted to be my friend. I guess my smoking made me more acceptable in her eyes. She didn't start a fight that morning and I was glad. I'm not saying we were besties that day, but she *was* to become my best friend in the world for a long time. She, my smoking teacher, Cindy, and I started sitting together at lunch. They were also in my study hall, which was in the cafeteria last period, so we sat together there as well.

I rarely studied in study hall. I chatted with my two friends. We could be loud sometimes, so the teacher would separate the three of us, but I loved hanging around with Becky and Cindy. They were both clowns and you never knew what they were going to do. Each was always trying to outdo the other, which made it interesting. They would try to see who could make us laugh more. One time, after the teacher separated us, I saw Becky and Cindy by the water bubbler. I knew something was up, so I left my seat to get a drink at the same fountain. As I approached, I could see Becky had a mouth full of water. She winked at me, then faced Cindy and slapped herself in her cheeks forcing the water to spurt out onto Cindy. I laughed until I thought I would pee my pants. It was so funny and I loved that they could make me laugh. Laughing was something I rarely did those days. Everything that happened took the happiness out of me, but sometimes, they would put a little of it back for a little while.

That day, the study hall teacher was not impressed with my laughing. She did not see what Becky did and was so mad, she yelled at me to come sit by her. When I got there, she pulled the chair out just as I leaned forward to grab it and I fell. I hurt my back and told her she had no right to cause me to hurt myself and that I was telling my mother what she did. She then slapped me right across the face and said, "Tell her this, too." If she had not been a teacher, I would have slapped her back. Instead I walked away fighting tears of embarrassment. I don't think I even bothered to tell my mother. I knew she wouldn't care. It's kind of strange that hurting my feelings would make me want to cry, but hitting me would not. I would rather take a beating any day than have my emotions messed with. I was beginning to hate all adults and how they all seemed to think they had a right to hit me.

Lunchtime was fun. I would eat fast or not at all most of the time because I spent my lunch money on cigarettes. I would rush to the back of the school to sneak cigarettes with my girlfriends. There were a couple of boys who liked to hang around looking for dead frogs to throw at us girls. I was not squeamish and I didn't mind frogs, but who wants frog guts on them? Not me! So, all of the girls would run, leaving the boys to think they were so fearless. What damn fools they were.

I loved that brief time in school where I felt like I fit in. It was like I finally belonged somewhere. It was one of the few times in my life I didn't feel so alone. Cindy and I were in the same English class, right after lunch. All the English classes were in a building next door to the school. All you had to do was go out one door, up a few steps, and you were there. Cindy and I were never in a rush to get to English class, but we were usually on time. I remember one day it started snowing, so Cindy suggested we take the long way to class. This meant we would go out the door on the other side of the cafeteria and walk all the way around the building. We were about ten minutes late as we walked slowly, enjoying the snow. When we got to class, we were sent to the principal's office with a slip that read something like, "Cindy Revere and Patricia Bennett were absent from class until they graced us with their presence after their afternoon stroll in the snow." We had to stay after school and write I will not be late for class two hundred times. If I could go back to that day I would do it again. First, the snow was beautiful and second, just thinking about it and what the teacher said still brings a smile to my face.

I started hanging out with Becky after school. My mother didn't like me at her house, but I was not forbidden to go there, so I did. Her mother worked so she was not home all day. I would go over there after school and weekends and hang out. We didn't do much but listen to the radio, try on clothes, fix each other's hair—girl stuff.

She had a brother who was a couple of years older, but he was usually out. He hung out at the bowling alley down the street with some other boys who were older than him. I was not allowed to hang out in the bowling alley, but sometimes on

Saturday night, I would go bowling with friends. I thought it was strange I never saw him or his friends bowl. I think they hung out in the room with the pinball machines. When he was home, he usually had the friends from the bowling alley with him. I never felt comfortable around them. They were a lot older than Becky and me. Other than her brother, who was fifteen, the others were all eighteen. Becky and I would just stay in her room when they were there, which was not very often.

One Saturday, early in the evening, I went to Becky's and her brother answered the door. He told me she was not there but would be right back and I should come in and wait. It was November and cold out. I really didn't want to walk all the way back home, so I went in. Once I got inside, I saw he had his friends there and there were cans of beer on the table. I didn't know what to do, so I sat down at the table. Her brother offered me some soda and poured me a glass. I think he put something in my soda because I felt so tired, like I had when I broke my arm. I vaguely remember being led up the flight of stairs. I was in and out of sleep like the day my sister taunted me after my broken arm. It felt like a bad dream as one scene blurred into the next. All I can say is that I knew they had done to me what Crooked teeth did. I was sure of that. I also was sure that I hated myself for going in that house that night. I also hated myself for not being able to stop them. From that point on I despised all boys. As far as I was concerned, they were all pigs. They were the meanest nastiest people in the world. From that day on I believed the male species was never to be trusted, that most of them were child molesters, rapists, and womanizers. I believed it to the core of my soul. It was not until I was an adult that I would find this belief challenged.

* * *

Those boys raped me in November of 1967. After all that happened to me that summer, I was just beginning to feel normal again. I was still sleeping in my clothes and baths were still a problem, but I was beginning to be able to laugh again;

something I never thought would ever happen.

Before the rape, I was enjoying school for the most part. I was going to the Midnight Hour with my girlfriends where we danced together, not with the boys. But what happened that November night plunged me into the darkest period of my life. I was secretly cutting my arms with razor blades. I had carved the word hate in capital letters on the knuckles of my left hand. Sometimes in school, I would just sit writing the word hate repeatedly on lined yellow paper. I would write it so much there were times I had to force myself to stop, thinking if I wrote it one more time, I would go crazy. I was completely consumed with the word hate. I was walking the streets at night sometimes hoping I would meet someone who would kill me.

I had stomach aches that would last for weeks. The first one was in July, when one day I punched Rusty and he punched me in the stomach. A few days later I got the worst stomachache of my life. It lasted a full week. I stayed in the house the whole time on the couch until I got better.

When school started, the stomach aches began interfering, keeping me out. That got my mother's attention. She knew I wanted to go to school to be with my friends, and knew I was not a crier but was crying all the time because I was in really bad pain. I think she realized that if I was crying so much, something was seriously wrong. She decided to take me to the emergency room.

I was admitted to the hospital for four days. The doctor said I had something called gastritis. I had no idea what it was, only that I wanted it gone. My stomach was in constant pain. Gastritis is inflammation of the lining of the stomach. Apparently, you can get it from injury as well as stress, excessive alcohol, and overuse of certain medications and other things. Back then, I didn't connect Rusty's punching me in the stomach to the first time I had it, but I do now. I think the stress from being raped caused me to have the gastritis that put me in the hospital. Unlike with my broken arm, I didn't put up a fuss when the doctor said he wanted to put me in the hospital. Nor did I fight the medicine. I was in far too much pain and just wanted the pain to stop.

My mother did not visit me when I was in the hospital, which made me feel bad. Instead, she sent two of my sisters with some coloring books and small puzzles to give to me. I loved to color and still do.

One night around midnight, I heard the nurses talking loud to someone in the hallway. Then my dad came into the room. He said he just got home from work and found out I was in here. He was a trucker, then, and on the road a lot. It looked like he had tears in his eyes. He told me he was sorry that I was in the hospital sick and handed me a huge bag of Christmas candy. I remember wondering where he got Christmas candy in November. I was glad he cared about me and wanted to see me, but felt ashamed because I could tell he had been drinking a lot and realized the nurses probably knew as well. I don't remember him staying a long time, or what, if anything, I said to him. After he left, I cried myself to sleep. I cried because I knew he would probably fight with my mother when he went home. I cried because he loved me, and I needed him more than anything in the world, but he was an alcoholic and as much as he wanted to help, he couldn't. I was not even sure I deserved him to love me, and I cried because I felt so alone. I had so many feelings that night and spent so much of it in tears.

This was not the first time I had been in the hospital. I had been hospitalized two other times in my life. One time when I was an infant which I don't remember, and one time when I was three years old.

I was hospitalized for a few days because, for a few weeks, I was having trouble talking. My mother said I would try to tell her something, but my words would trail off, getting softer and softer until my mouth was moving, but nothing was coming out. She said she brought me to the doctor and he talked to me and the same thing happened. I would start talking my voice would trail off to nothing but moving lips so I was hospitalized so they could put me in the operating room for a procedure to look down my throat at my vocal cords.

This hospitalization is my first real memory of my life. I can remember vividly my mother undressing me, putting a hospital gown on me, and putting my clothes in a brown paper bag. For some reason, when I saw my clothes go in a bag, I knew she was leaving me there. I remember crying and crying, but otherwise remember only bits and pieces about the stay, like the blood pressure cuff because it hurt. And I remember being in a crib with a net on it, though I didn't understand why. I was not a baby and wanted to stand up but couldn't because of the net. The nurse told me if I promised not to climb out again, she would take it off, but I must stay in it no matter what. I agreed I would not climb out.

I remember them bringing me to a room where there were other kids and a television. The *Mickey Mouse Club* was on and I sat there watching it while crying and watching for my mother. I wanted to go home and didn't know why she was not coming to get me. Other mothers were coming to see their kids, but not mine. She did not return until the day I was released.

The doctor told my mother they did not find anything wrong with my voice and had no explanation as to why I could not talk right. He said that since they could not find the cause, there was nothing they could do to help, and it would probably resolve on its own. Apparently, eventually, it did. I don't remember leaving the hospital. This hospital stay is something that came back to me at the age of thirty-six in 1990. I will get into that later on.

Nine

I don't remember leaving the hospital, or Thanksgiving or Christmas that year. I believe after my hospital stay I was just back to every day blending into the next. The next time I remember was in January. I stopped by Becky's on the way to school like I usually did. Her brother was never there mornings, so I knew it was safe to stop there. She wasn't ready, so I went in to wait. She had this bright idea that we should skip school.

I previously only skipped once, when I lived in Boston in the sixth grade. My mother made me wear a pair of knee socks that had a hole in them. I was embarrassed and told her I was not going to go to school, and I didn't. I went to the house where I babysat and she let me hang out there for the day. When I got home, my mother asked me where I had been during catechism class that day. The other kids told her I didn't go. I told her I skipped. I'm not sure she realized I skipped school as well, but I didn't get in trouble. Remembering how I didn't get in trouble in Boston the time I skipped school, I figured I could do it again and get away with it, so I agreed to skip school with Becky that day.

When I went home at the usual time, my mother was there, and she was mad. She demanded to know where I was all day. Instead of telling her the truth, that Becky and I skipped school, I claimed I was at school. That's when she told me the school called her to see why I was not there. I continued to lie, saying I was late because Becky was not ready when I got there. This was not unusual as we were late all the time. I tried to get her to believe I was on the absent list just because I was late, but it did not work. My mother was getting madder and madder and kept telling me to tell her the truth. She said if I told the truth, I would be in less trouble but I was scared to death. She had my father's black garrison belt in her hand and I knew I was going to get hit no matter what I said. I also knew she didn't like me going to Becky's, so I figured if I told the truth it would be worse. I decided she was never going to pry the truth out of me and stuck to my story. Other than my older sister I'm not sure if anybody else was in the living room with us, but whoever was, she told them to leave.

Karen left the room and my mother pushed our German Shepherd out with her. She closed both doors and began to swing the belt at me. She was swinging it like a crazy person not caring where it landed, but with purpose. I felt it hit my leg. She was screaming for me to take my jeans off. I heard her say she was going to scar my legs for life. I was so terrified I didn't know what to do. But I knew I was not taking my jeans off. I was positive about that. No matter what she said that was not going to happen. I dropped to the floor curled myself into a ball tucking my arms, legs and head under me as best I could. The only place left exposed for her to hit was my back. I don't know how long she wailed on me. I kept begging for her to stop. I was promising I would be an angel from now on. Finally she stopped and yelled, "Damn right you will. Now get upstairs."

I don't remember my feet hitting the stairs. I just remember being in the room I shared with my sisters and feeling the tears streaming down my face. I was completely stunned. Karen came into the room and asked, "What did she do to you?" I turned around and lifted my shirt so she could see my back. She began to weep so bitterly it sent shivers down my spine. I figured it must be bad to make her cry since we didn't get along. I didn't know she even cared about me. Other than that one question, not another word was spoken between us about what happened for over 30 years.

As adults there was only one time, we talked about it. She told me how devastated she was during the entire ordeal. She was in the next room and could hear everything. She didn't know what to do and said she felt helpless, afraid, and angry about what our mother was doing to me. We have never talked about it again because it is too painful for her. I completely understood how helpless she felt. I knew the feeling well, having experienced it more times in my life than I care to remember. Times like when my dad fought with my mother; when he would be drunk and throw one of our cats at a wall; when he would lose his temper at one of my brothers; when my mother beat my dad with the clothes rack; when I was raped and molested. Yes, I knew the feeling well. Along with anger, it became my constant companion. It became about the only other feeling I knew. For so long, I was angry, helpless, or empty.

* * *

About a week after the beating, I asked my mother for permission to go to the laundry with Becky after school. I didn't give my mother a time because I was not sure what time we were going. After school, I went to Becky's house and we hung out until her mother got out of work and got the laundry together. Since they didn't have a washer, they didn't get to do laundry every day like my mother, so there was a lot of it to do. We left around six o'clock and finished it around nine o'clock and I left for home. It was about one-half mile to Becky's house, then another mile and a quarter to my house. I didn't even stop at Becky's, just walked straight home. It was the middle of January. There was a lot of snow on the ground and it was bitter cold outside so I stayed on the road walking as fast as I could. I got home around nine forty-five.

When I got home, the shit hit the fan. My mother was not working that night and was pissed, demanding to know where I had been. I told her the truth; that I was with Becky and her mother at the laundry. She started screaming at me, "Don't tell me you were at the laundry until almost ten o'clock at night. Laundry doesn't take that long to do." Before I could say anything, she grabbed me by the hair, slapped my face, then shoved me against the refrigerator. She had me by the hair and was slapping me across the face when suddenly someone grabbed my arm and pulled me away from her. It was my dad. He was home and he was drunk. He pulled me down the hallway, opened the door said, "Get the hell out of here before she kills you." He shoved me out the door, then pulled my coat off the banister and threw it out behind me. After he threw me out, I stood there for a minute, completely stunned, not knowing what to do. Then I picked my coat up, put it on, and started walking away from our house as fast as I could.

I know this might sound strange, but I felt free. I started running down the street, headed toward Becky's house and wondering what would happen if my father changed his mind and came after me. I didn't want that to happen, so instead of going straight down the road where it was easier to walk. I decided to run behind the line of houses on the right side of the street where I could not be seen from the road. Although that meant I would be running in knee deep snow, I didn't care. I didn't want to be seen. I know for sure I didn't have boots on. I am not sure if I had shoes on or not. I have always believed I did not, but it didn't matter to me because I was free, and I wanted it to stay that way.

It seemed like I knocked on the door forever before someone answered it. When Becky let me in, I told her and her mother what happened when I got home. Her mother told me I had to go to the police station and tell them about my father kicking me out, so, after I got warm, they gave me some boots to put on. Then my friend and I went to the police station. At the police station, they said they needed to call the juvenile officer in to talk to me. They put us in a room to wait, but it was not long before Mr. McCarley came into the small room. I told him what happened that night. I then told him what had happened the week before when I skipped school. I lifted the back of my shirt so he could see I was telling him the truth about what happened the previous week. I hadn't even told Becky and wanted someone to know the truth. I knew the welts and bruises were still there. I looked at them every day in the mirror. Mr. McCarley told me to go back to Becky's for the night, then come to the police station in the morning.

When I arrived at the police station in the morning, they put me in a room all alone I stayed there the better part of the day until the Juvenile officer came to get me. He led me to a chair outside a small courtroom and told me to wait there.

I saw my mother come into the police station. She had on her long black coat. She looked so small and sad. I was so mad I felt like I could spit on her. It pains me to say I am not sure that I didn't. The juvenile officer returned to get me. He led me into a small courtroom. There were not many of us in that court room. The judge, my mother, my grandmother, the juvenile officer, me, and someone taking notes.

I remember the judge saying something about me going to live with my grandmother. I heard myself say I don't want to. He told me if I didn't want to go with my gram, he would have to send me to reform school. I said, "That's fine by me."

I guess I didn't really care anymore what happened to me. I was full of self-hatred. I blamed myself for everything; for what happened in July because I had let them in; for what happened in the gas station because of my fear; for what happened in November because I went in the house; for lying to my mother about skipping school, which set all this in motion.

Truth be known, I really wanted to go with my nana. I loved her dearly. But I knew if I went with her, my family would call my mother unfit. How could I let that happen? As mad as I was at my mother, I could not let her be blamed for something that was my fault. I have always had a fierce sense of loyalty and fairness. I guess a part of me believed I deserved to go to reform school since I had lied, which put all this in motion.

I don't remember much of what happened after that. I vaguely remember a sheriff driving me to the reform school. It was dark when we arrived. Nor do I remember feeling much. I think I just felt empty.

The first memory I have is standing in a dimly lit bathroom, shaking and wondering why I had let myself get into this mess. I could have avoided it if only I had gone to my grandmother's house. A middle-age woman was peering right at me telling me to take off my clothes. How could I? First, I was extremely modest. Second, what happened in July made taking my clothes off almost impossible for me, even when I was alone.

She didn't care, just said, "Get them off."

I turned away so I could not see her watching me and quickly undressed. She passed me a plain white nightgown and house coat like the ones you get in the hospital. She sprayed some crap that smelled bad all through my hair then wrapped my head in a towel. Then we walked down a short hallway with rooms on each side. The doors all had a small, six-inch-square window in them. We walked to the last room on the left where the door was open. She told me to get in there, gave me a small shove, then shut the door, locked it, glanced in the window at me, and was gone.

The bed was bolted to the floor in front of a large, opaque window that was completely covered with a wire grate. Clearly, they didn't want anyone to open it and leave. Since this was a second floor it didn't seem to make much sense, but at the time, my only thought was, *whatever!* There was a tiny doorless closet with a stainless-steel bed pan. I shuddered. I could not imagine having to use it with no privacy. The entire room could be seen from the tiny window in the door. Anybody could look in, so I had no intention of using that bed pan, ever. As far as I was concerned, I had other options — peeing my pants being one of them. At the time, it seemed like the only option. There were times it felt like my teeth were floating, but my attitude was, let them float away. I was not using that thing, period.

I sat down on the bed and the flood gate opened. I cried like the night I cried in the hospital. When I was younger, the only thing that would make me cry was when my mother said mean things to me. But her mean words no longer had that effect.

These days, I could not have cared less what she said. As far as I was concerned, she was a stupid, mean, hateful bitch and I was glad to be away from her. So here I was, this tough-as-nails girl sitting in a locked, Reform School room, crying my heart out, not knowing what was going to happen next. Of course, that was nothing new. Lately, the big question for me was always, what would happen next? I could never be sure. Still, I thought, *Who cares? Nothing could be worse than what's already happened to me!*

* * *

I was scared as hell all the time. I learned I was not as tough as I thought I was; that I could no longer protect myself. Boys were stronger than me, and though I thought I was stronger than my mother, I would never have raised my hands to her. I just didn't have that in me. She was my mother and no matter what, you never raised your hands against your parent. Everything that happened this past year showed me I was not as bomb-proof as I once thought. I now felt defenseless most of the time and had nobody I could turn to. I didn't trust a soul, including myself. I hated my mother, but felt such a deep hate for myself it scared me.

I prayed a lot during that time. I didn't know much about God, only what I was taught in my childhood — that He loved us enough He sent Jesus to die for us. Though I was not sure about that, I *was* pretty sure He still hated boldness. I had not forgotten how bold I was, but as I did when I was seven, hoped He would forgive me and that He might love me even though I was bold. What I didn't know was that, as afraid of God as I was, He was looking out for me the whole time. My father threw me out of the house trying to protect me from my mother that January night. I guess he didn't know what else to do. I knew my dad loved me and always wanted to help me, but his alcoholism prevented him from being able to. Little did he or I know that when he threw me out that night something good would come from it.

* * *

King James Bible - Psalm 27:10
When my father and my mother forsake me, then the LORD
will take me up.

* * *

God had me in the palm of his hand. Reform school was
going to be the safest place in the world for me. Of course, I
didn't know it back then. But looking back, I can see how He
used it to protect me from everything that was happening in
my life. There were so many things going on that were out of
control, including myself. I needed His divine intervention and
protection. God can use all things for our benefit. He loved me
and had His hand holding tight to mine.

* * *

King James Bible - Psalm 27:5
For in the time of trouble he shall hide me in his pavilion: in the
secret of his tabernacle shall he hide me; he shall set me up
upon a rock.

* * *

I must have cried myself to sleep that night. I was awakened
by voices. I looked up and saw 2 half faces in the window of
the door and ran to the door. They were asking me where I
came from and what I did wrong to get there. Answering the
first question was easy I was from Dover. The second was not a
simple one. I had not really done anything wrong. I didn't
think they would believe that, so I didn't answer that question
right away. Eventually I would tell them about the beating and
my dad kicking me out, but not that day. I had a lot of
questions myself.

How long would I have to stay in this room? They told me a
couple of days. How long will this towel have to stay on my
head? Someone would be there soon to take me to get the crap
washed out. I was happy to hear that. The smell was so strong I

was starting to feel sick. What time was breakfast? I don't remember the answer but I was hungry, not having eaten anything since the morning before.

It was not long before a woman — they called them officers — came to get me. She led me down the long hall to the bathroom I was in the night before. There was a huge sink where she washed the crap out of my hair. Then she handed me a clean nightgown and housecoat, told me to take a bath, and left, locking the door behind her. As you know, I was not a bath person, but I felt so dirty from not being able to wash up since my dad had tossed me out the door three days ago. I ran the tub, climbed in, and submerged my head under the water. I sat there for a long time, surprised by how good it felt.

When I got out of the tub, I put on the clean nightgown and house coat, then sat on the floor waiting for the woman to come get me. As I sat there, I realized just how much Rusty and Crooked Teeth had taken from me. Thinking that in the past would have made me angry, but I felt so clean and good at that moment and was not going to let anything rob me of that feeling, least of all those two idiots. They were not going to take another thing from me ever again.

The woman came back and banged on the door to see if I was dressed. I said yes, she unlocked the door, and led me back down the hallway to the room I came from. Since it was daylight, I could see so much I did not notice the night before. The hall floor was tiled black and white. It was beautiful. You could see reflections of everything in it. I found it hard to believe these floors were walked on constantly. You could tell they were well cared for. I would soon learn they were washed, waxed, and buffed every Saturday, and buffed each day, as well. They had a huge housekeeping team — us girls. We were all expected to keep the place spotless, and I do mean spotless. The walls were paneled halfway up. I don't know what kind of wood it was, but it looked like Brazilian Cherry. It, too, was spotless, with not a speck of dust to be seen. The "housekeeping team" did their best to keep the place immaculate.

Soon after I was returned to my room, the officer came back

with a breakfast tray. I think it was oatmeal, toast, orange juice, and fruit. I remember thinking, *Wow a well-balanced breakfast!* I was starving, so I know I ate it.

Not long after I finished, a girl looked in my window. She was on the housekeeping team that day and was dusting the baseboard near my room. She told me there was another girl from Dover there and that her name was Darlene.

That day was a long one for me. I had nothing to do but sit and think. Only my meals and people looking in the window to catch a glimpse of the new girl from Dover broke up my day.

Eventually Darlene came to the window. She wanted to know how old I was, what grade I was in and what school I went to. Apparently, she had a brother in the Junior High. He was in seventh grade like me and I knew him. She seemed happy I knew her brother. Although I didn't like boys, I let her know I thought he was cute and it wasn't a lie. He was a cute kid and very sweet. She smiled when I said that.

I'm not sure if it was me being from Dover or thinking her brother was cute or both that made her treat me well, but she did. She took me under her wing, which was good for me since she was the oldest, toughest girl in this place. Everyone looked up to her and Wanda, another girl she hung out with. Once I was released from security, they let me hang out with them. I was glad, because I figured nobody would start trouble with me knowing they would have to answer to Darlene. I was the youngest and smallest girl in the place and was given a nickname. I have no idea who decided I needed it, but everybody called me Peewee. Although I didn't really like the name, I must admit I felt special when they called me that. These girls—most of them—were nice to me.

It is kind of strange I was sent there because I didn't want to live with my grandmother. The other girls all did something like run away, shoplift, or something else wrong. Still, it seemed odd to me that I felt like I belonged there, with them, but it was a good feeling. I liked feeling like I fit in, and these girls became my family.

The new room would be mine for the remainder of my stay.

I learned the judge sentenced me to thirty days. The people here called it ADC for Awaiting District Court.

My room was in the security section. There were three hallways—Security, West Hall, and East Hall. An officer sat at the desk at the junction of the three halls. Security hall had two sections. One had four rooms on each side, plus a bathroom and a nurse's office. The other section had only two rooms one on each side. Security rooms all had a window in them so the occupant could be checked on during the night. If a girl was only here for thirty days, like me, she stayed there the whole time. If she would be there for longer, they kept her in security until they became familiar with her. Then she would be moved to a regular room on East or West Hall.

East and West hall were long and had a lot of rooms on each side, but I don't know how many. West Hall also had a special room for a teen who just had a baby to stay in after the baby was born, but I don't think her baby stayed there, too. I knew about one girl who stayed in it, but I never saw a baby. It seemed like she was there for a few days, then gone.

West Hall also had a huge bathroom with a bathtub with a shower on the right that was enclosed with special glass you could not see through. If you took a left when you entered, there were two more baths like the first one. If you walked straight there were three toilet stalls on each side. After the stalls there were three sinks on each side. This was where all the girls washed up and brushed their teeth each morning. Baths were required each night, so it was a busy place. Your baths were as quick as you could make them; no dilly-dallying.

The bathrooms were kept as spotless as the rest of the place. You were required to wash out the tub and sink after use and wipe them dry. They were also scrubbed each day by the house cleaning crew—us. They taught us how they expected the bathrooms cleaned right down to making sure the chrome shined.

When you finished a job, an officer would check what you did. If it was not done to their specification, you had to repeat it again. We were graded on everything we did. I used to think half those officers probably didn't even keep their own houses that clean; that they were probably slobs. But they sure expected perfection out of us and they would get it out of me. Since the third grade and that poem and awesome teacher, I was always a person who did my best.

I could always find someone in authority who didn't like me, and that place was no different. One officer didn't like me, I don't know why, and would look for ways to get me. One time, when I just finished dusting the baseboards in a hall, the buffer went by and sprayed stuff from the floor on it. The officer said I didn't do a good enough job, that I had to repeat it. I was so mad I muttered under my breath, "Bitch." When she asked me what I said, I just looked at her, but one of the girls told her I called her a bitch. I got locked up for the rest of the day. That happened during my second stay here. That officer and I would butt heads all the time, now and when I would return for a longer stay.

* * *

Reform School was an unofficial name. I learned the real name was the State Industrial School. I guess us girls being industrious was the industrial part of this place. Otherwise it was just a state lock up for bad kids or kids, like me, whose parents didn't give a crap about them.

Days started early when the lights came on at six o'clock in the morning and ended with lights off at nine o'clock at night. The lights were our alarm clock. The girls who worked in the kitchen were awakened each morning at five-thirty by the night officer. Upon waking, we had to strip our bed and turn our mattress over. To make sure we did it, we had to stand with our mattress standing on its side, waiting for the officer to go by before you dropped it down. Lord forbid your mattress didn't get turned. After we washed up and brushed our teeth, we went back to our rooms to make our beds. Then we were required to sweep, wash, and buff the floor in our room on our hands and knees. Next we'd go to the dining room to eat, followed by whatever your assignment was for the day—

housekeeping, laundry, or sewing room.

There was a lot to do in this place and each week, your work assignment would change. Many of the officers really cared about and looked out for us. The one who was on the desk was usually the one in charge of housekeeping each day.

As best I can remember, girls who were there for thirty days or less only got put in housekeeping, the job I hated the most because that officer was the one I butted heads with all the time. I'll call her Mrs. Grumpy. She didn't like me at all. I dreaded being stuck with her for the day. There were times I wanted to ask her who peed in her Cheerios that morning. I never did, but sure wanted to. She was the officer who took my blankets away for a few days at a time if I was caught sleeping with my head under the blankets. That happened at least three times. I always slept with my head under the blankets at home. It was a habit I got into from being cold at night. I was told it was too dangerous for me to sleep that way because I was so small that when they looked in the window, if they could not see my head, it was hard to tell I was there. In case of a fire, they needed to be sure they could see my head. I eventually learned to keep my head uncovered, but the learning process was hard for me. I didn't like being cold those nights they took my blanket.

I began to learn some restraint with my mouth. I learned the consequences for saying something you should not was usually lockup and I hated being locked in my room because there was nothing to do but think. I hated thinking because most of the time, what I thought about was all that transpired in my life over this last year, things that were very unpleasant for me to revisit. I also learned to answer with "yes ma'am" or "no ma'am" when spoken to. It was required, not optional, and it was difficult to get in the habit, but eventually I did.

Meals were not optional either. You were assigned to a table and the assignment was permanent. I hated where I had to sit. It was directly in front of the Officers' table. During meals, I was face to face with the officer at the table, usually the officer on hall duty with us upstairs, which was usually Mrs. Grumpy.

We lined up to get our meals and walked single file through the kitchen to be served. We could tell the person serving how much we wanted. Then, depending on who the server was, you would be happy or want to rip her head off. If she liked you, no worries. If she did not, she could make your life hell by giving you more of what you hated and less of what you liked. We were required to eat everything on our plates, period, like it or not, so it was important to get along with the server.

Sometimes, when the Officer was not looking my way, I would hide something I hated under my napkin on my plate and try to get that napkin in the trash without being noticed. Most of the time it worked, but not always. If it didn't work, they gave you more of what you threw away and made a mental note to watch you more closely. Every morning, they made us drink a half-cup of coffee. You could have milk in it, but no sugar and I hated it. I liked the tea I had at home sometimes, but never before had a cup of coffee and didn't care if I ever had another one after that place. I never learned to like it. Today, though I drink decaf from time to time, real coffee is just not for me.

The meals here were balanced. We had fruit every meal, which I loved because I love fruit. We didn't get lots of fruit in my house, mostly oranges or apples, but I loved pears, peaches, grapes, and plums. White cherries, stewed apricots, and prunes I hated. I couldn't choke down a prune, but lucky for me there was a girl at my table who loved them. When Officer Grumpy was not looking, I would dump mine into her bowl. I would make it up to her by eating something for her she didn't like.

We had structure there. Two nights a week, we got to go down to the craft room in the basement. Some of the girls didn't like crafts so they would go to a TV room. Wherever we went, we were supervised by an officer. The one in the craft room was a very sweet older lady. She had the patience of a saint. She would teach us how to knit or crochet. I loved the craft room and was learning to knit. I started practicing by trying to make a headband. It was growing wider as I went along and didn't look anything like a head band. It was one inch wide at one end then three inches on the other! When someone asked what it was, I told them it looked like a shawl for a Barbie doll. They never questioned how I figured out how to make it. Eventually, I threw it away and made up my mind I was going to do it right. I wanted to become a good knitter. I could see others working on really nice stuff like sweaters and I dreamed of making a sweater.

On my return visit here, I would do just that—make a sweater. I absolutely loved knitting and still do. It made me feel good to be able to create something. Knitting was something I could be good at if I tried hard enough. There were so many wrong things in my life, so much I was blamed for, that I was not sure anymore what was my fault and what wasn't. I felt worthless most of the time but knitting gave me something to concentrate on other than all the crap in my head. It was something I could feel good about and God knows I sure needed it.

One-night, while I was in the craft room, my stomach began to hurt like it had when I was in the hospital. The pain was so bad I didn't know what to do. I went to the officer and told her my stomach hurt bad and I didn't want to stay here. I asked if I could go in the TV room. I knew the chairs were more comfortable there and I would not have to do anything but sit. She let me leave and I went straight there. About half-an-hour later, the fire alarm went off. It was so loud it hurt my ears.

They brought us out of the TV room to the large foyer with a door to the back yard. They also brought the girls up from the craft room. We were just standing there listening to the alarm. I could smell smoke, but didn't know where the smell was coming from. Some of the girls were screaming at the top of their lungs but their screaming made no sense to me. There was nothing to be afraid of. We were standing right near a door to the outside and although it was locked, I was not afraid. I knew they would open it and bring us outside if they needed to. The alarm blared for quite a while until the fire department came and shut it off. Then the officers brought us upstairs to get ready for bed. All we had to do was brush our teeth, so it was quick.

After bed check and my door was locked, I usually fell asleep quickly. That night was no different. My stomachache was easing up and I was exhausted from the day, so I went to sleep easy. I no sooner fell asleep than was awakened by the light in my room. At first, I thought it was morning. Then I saw two men and one woman officer standing in my room. I was startled to see them. I didn't know who the men were or why they were in my room. They said they wanted me to tell them about the fire in the laundry room that night. I wondered why they were asking me. How would I know? I didn't know anything about a fire in the laundry room. Never having been there, I didn't even know where the laundry room was.

Apparently, there was a fire there which is what set the alarm off that night, which was news to me. I only knew the alarm went off and we could smell smoke so I told them I didn't know.

They said, "Yes you do. It was you that started it."

I was so paralyzed with fear I could hardly speak. I had no idea what they were talking about. I didn't start a fire. They said I was friends with Darlene and Wanda and the three of us planned the fire while in the school room each day. I told them I didn't go to school with them. I was an ADC girl. I only went to school for an hour each afternoon. They said they knew for sure I was involved, that I was the first to leave the craft room before it was started. I explained that I had a bad stomachache and went right to the TV room when I left. They said they didn't believe me and that they would get to the bottom of it. I was scared to death and didn't sleep at all that night because they believed I started a fire.

In the morning, I learned Darlene and Wanda started the fire after I left to go up to the TV room. Each of them got permission to go to the bathroom and went to the laundry room and started the fire. Now they were in two of the four rooms in the basement for solitary confinement.

I didn't even know they had such a thing there. I had no idea there were rooms in the basement. Someone pointed them out to me the next time we went to the craft room. They were awful looking big green steel doors with a window like the ones in security. They were not far from the bathroom and I was surprised I never noticed them before. I guess I was not very observant when using the rest room. I went there and back and never looked around, probably because I hated basements. They brought back too many bad memories about Crooked Teeth and Rusty.

I went to the door of both rooms when I went to the bathroom. Darlene was indeed in one and Wanda in another. They looked horrible. There were iron beds that didn't look like they had mattresses. All they had was a skimpy blanket, and the floors were just dirt. I cried when I saw my friends in there. I could not believe they put them in a place like that. I heard they didn't give them much food either, just the basics with no fruit or dessert.

Darlene and Wanda told the men how they planned the fire, as well as how they stole a lighter from one of the officers. They told them I didn't know a thing about it and I thank God they told the truth. What a coincidence I had a stomachache that evening. I left the room just before the two of them went to the laundry room.

I cried myself to sleep that night, partly because I was sad for my friends who were locked in that awful basement, but also, because I knew if they had not told the truth, I could be in there with them. That was a terrifying thought to say the least. I still shudder when I think about the events of that night, and how grateful I am God protected me.

* * *

King James Bible - Deuteronomy 31:6
Be strong and of a good courage, fear not, nor be afraid of them: for the LORD thy God, he it is that doth go with thee; he will not fail thee, nor forsake thee.

* * *

I left reform school a few days later. It was mid-February. I don't remember the ride to court or court itself. Nor do I remember anything about seeing my family. What I do remember about that day is the girls telling me at breakfast, "You'll be back," and me telling them I would not, that I hated the place.

Ten

I don't remember much of anything after I was released until the weekend before my fourteenth birthday. I remember that because I asked my mother about the birthday party we were all promised when we turned fourteen. My birthday was going to be on Monday so I figured if there was going to be a party it would have to be this weekend or next. Then Mom made it crystal clear I was not having a party and I made it clear to her if that was true, I would run away on my birthday.

Monday, March twenty-fifth, I got up as usual and got ready for school. I decided to ask my mother one more time about the birthday party. I wanted to make sure there was not a surprise party planned. She told me the same thing she said all weekend. I was not going to have a party. I let her know I was not coming home, that I was running away. I don't think she believed me. I was so tired of being treated badly by her. I was tired of everybody and everything. I knew when I walked out the door I would not be back for a very long time. I had no idea where I would go or what I would do, only that I was running away. That was all the thought I gave it. So out the door I walked that March morning in 1968. It was my fourteenth birthday. I would not return through those doors until November twelfth.

I met up with my friends as usual at Dean's place. I don't

recall how I met him, but he was an eighteen year old guy who had his own apartment. It was right over the cab stand where my mother worked. Dean had a girlfriend who was seventeen, and although my friends and I were younger, they didn't mind us hanging out with them. Mornings before school and sometimes after school we would all meet there. We didn't do much. It was mostly a place to hang out, smoke cigarettes, and stay warm.

My mother forbade me to be there, but I could not have cared less what my mother said anymore. I was going to do what I wanted to do from now on, and what I wanted was to hang out there with my friends.

One time, before I ran away, we had a huge pillow fight at Dean's place and one of the pillows broke and feathers went everywhere. I was wearing a dress made with some material they stuck to and was covered in them. We brushed off as many of the feathers as we could with a whisk broom, but there were still some left. That night, when I got home from the library, my mother lit into me. She wouldn't believe I was at the library. She started hitting me, calling me names like whore and stuff when she saw feathers. I tried to explain what happened, but she would not listen. Nothing had changed between us since reform school. She was still the same never-listening, always-blaming bitch.

So here I was, running away. I decided I better go to school first, then run away, and went to school like normal. After school, I went to a friend's house. Her mother was at work and I stayed there visiting all evening. Around one thirty in the morning, my friend said I would have to sleep in the car in the backyard because her mother would be home soon. I went outside, lit a cigarette, and climbed into the back seat of the car. It was sort of a junk car and didn't run.

That was how I spent my fourteenth birthday — so different from how I dreamed it would be. I dreamed it would be like the one that Karen had, with all her friends, aunts, and uncles there, and our parents celebrating, dancing, and all. I felt so robbed. It was like a knife to my heart, but I was not going to cry over it. I was too angry about everything. My mother could go straight to hell and she could take my father with her as far as I was concerned. I didn't care that he made me promise that day when I was five years old that I would come to him when I had a problem and not run away. I think I knew when I was five he could not help me and I sure as hell knew it now. When he threw me out in January, he showed me how much he could not help me. When I needed him the most, the only time he was there when my mother was slapping me around, he tossed me to the dogs. I didn't matter to either of them, so to hell with them. That was how I felt.

I didn't sleep that night. I chain smoked all night, trying to keep warm. It is a good thing I had a full pack of cigarettes. They were probably what kept me awake and from freezing to death.

I was so happy when the sun came up and headed for Dean's apartment to get warm and meet my friends. I knew I could not go to school today because they would be looking for me. My friend Debbie was at Dean's and said she would run away with me, which I thought was cool. I was happy I was not alone. Debbie and I hung out in the woods all day. That night we went to a five and dime-like store called Sawyer Mills. Debbie said we should steal some rings, so we did. I never before stole anything like that, only devil dogs when I was a little kid back in Boston. I stole a ring for each finger and wish I could say I felt guilty doing it, but I didn't. I didn't care about anything. The only feeling I had was anger.

Debbie suggested we hitchhike to Rochester to her sister's house. It was the first time I ever hitchhiked, but she had hitched before so I said ok since we were together. We walked about five miles toward Rochester before we got a ride. Some middle age guy in a jeep picked us up. He said he was headed to Rochester and would drop us off at a Cumberland Farms that was right before her sister's street. He was as good as his word and dropped us right where he said he would.

Debbie's sister said we could spend the night. It never entered my mind that she might turn us in. I think I was just too tired to think straight. Having been awake since the morning before, I fell asleep on the couch almost as soon as I sat down. It was now around nine o'clock at night.

When I woke up in the morning, her sister told us we had to turn ourselves in; that if we did, we would not get in trouble. She said she called the police and asked, and they said if she saw us, to tell us we would not get in trouble, so we told her she could call the police for us. They were there quick.

They put us in the back of a police car. Since we were in Rochester, they said another police car would be meeting us in Somersworth. Then Dover would meet the Somersworth Police. That was how we got back to Dover.

I thought they would bring us home, but they brought us to the station. They put us in the same room I was in back in January. Then we went to court. I remember my mother being there. When the judge said I was going to reform school, I was sick to death. I didn't want to go back there.

After court, they put me in an actual jail cell to wait for the sheriff. It was not long before they brought Debbie down to the cell and put her in with me. She had to go to reform school, too. I felt bad because I knew it was my fault. She only ran away because of me. I lay down and started kicking the wall and screaming. I only wanted to be put in a foster home. I was screaming my head off and kicking the wall for a few minutes when Debbie just burst out laughing. I didn't think it was funny and told her she would not be laughing when we got to reform school.

An old sheriff came to bring us. He had his wife with him and they were nice. They stopped at a store and asked us if we wanted anything. We told them cigarettes. I was amazed they bought them for us. We smoked as many as we could all the way to reform school. It was around five o'clock when we arrived. Poor Debbie had no idea what to expect. I at least knew what would happen.

I was in the same, dimly-lit bathroom with the same officer, the one who didn't like me. She did all the things, like put the crap on my head, wrap it in a towel, and make me take my clothes off before giving me the same white nightgown and same house coat. The only difference this time was I didn't get put in security. I was put in West Hall, room ten. I guess the place was full. Debbie *was* put in security.

I supposed the girls would find out when they looked in Debbie's window that she came here from Dover with me. News spreads fast in a place like that. It was not long before people were talking to me through the door. I could hear some of them laughing, saying, "I told you that you would be back." It was strange being back there after only being home a month. I didn't want to be there and could not believe it.

There were loudspeakers they used to call out names of girls they needed to come to the office for something. I heard them call some familiar names, names of people that left just before me and others I knew were due to leave just after me. It was like a reunion. There were four or five of us who were back and though I felt bad for them and me, I was glad I would have some girls here I knew well.

We had all been in security together. I was not an ADC girl this time; I was here for the long hall although I didn't realize that right away. In fact, it was not until the day Debbie went home that I found out I had been sentenced to six and a half months. That was a really bad day for me.

Some of the girls were taunting me about how my friend was leaving but I wasn't. I can remember one girl standing in front of the nurse's office in the security hallway. The officer was at the desk as usual. This girl was saying mean stuff to me. I told her to shut up and leave me alone. She said something like she was not going to shut up and what was I going to do about it. I told her if she didn't shut her mouth, I would punch her. She said she didn't think I would dare do it with the nurse and the officer right there watching. I flew to her and punched her right in the mouth. I think she was shocked but I had nothing to lose. I knew I had to stick up for myself right then or be bullied the rest of my stay there, especially since I had no friend to protect me this stay. I was not going to let some little twit think I was too afraid to stick up for myself. Besides, I was tired of being picked on by her and I was having a really bad day. It was not a good time for someone to push me.

I learned Darlene was in State Prison for starting the fire. Wanda was too young to go to state prison, so she was locked up here with time added. She would leave this place the same day I would, but it was not going to be that day. I was going to be there for the next seven and a half months.

Of course, I was locked up in security for punching the girl. I was so mad I pulled the mattress off the bed and put it against the door so nobody could look in the window at me. It was not long until an officer I didn't know came to the door—Mrs. Myers. She banged on the door and demanded I take the mattress down. I told her to kiss my ass. She then made it clear I was to take that mattress down immediately or else she was going to come in there and kick *my* ass. Something about her tone told me she meant what she said and I pulled the mattress down. She looked at me through the window and I think she was surprised when she saw me.

We never met on my last visit and I think how small and young I was caused her to feel compassion for me. She opened the door and talked to me. She asked about the fight, so I told her the girl was making fun of me because my friend was leaving that day and I had just learned I was not leaving with her and had to stay. I told her the girl was laughing at me and daring me to do something, so I did. She said she understood why I punched the girl, but I could not be fighting anymore. She said if I could behave myself for the next couple of hours, she would get me out of there at dinner time. I didn't really believe her and was shocked when she did it.

That evening, she got me out at dinner time. She said she was going to have me put on kitchen and laundry duty from now on, and that she wanted to keep an eye on me. I no longer had to be in housekeeping during the week, only Saturdays when all the girls did housekeeping.

I liked this woman from the moment I met her. She listened to me about the fight and I was not used to someone caring about what happened. I was used to being blamed and not listened to. She took the time to listen and that made her great in my mind.

The next morning, I started in the kitchen with Mrs. Story, and after morning kitchen duty, I was put in the laundry with Mrs. Myers as the officer. I loved both of those jobs.

The jobs were demanding, but the two people in charge were reasonable people. Not all the officers there were fair, but these were. They all had their pets. I was not a person who usually became a pet, but I have to say I soon felt like I was one of Mrs. Myers pets. She had a couple of us. They were all tough like me and Wanda.

I thought when she said she wanted to keep her eye on me she meant to make sure I didn't cause trouble, but I discovered she wanted to look out for me. Looking back, I think she knew I was basically a good kid, but that I was reactive and could be pushed into trouble. I also think she knew the officer on housekeeping didn't like me and would look for ways to trip me up.

Mrs. Myers was awesome. Don't get me wrong—she was tough. You had to do what you were supposed to do and she didn't tolerate any crap, but she was fair. She was not the kind of officer who watched you like a hawk. She told you what she expected of you and left you to do it. She put her trust in you. I valued her trust more than anything. I personally believe the most valuable gift a person can give me or anyone is trust. It means more to me than anything. I value it more than gold.

One day, I asked Mrs. Myers her first name. She told me Eleanor. She thought it was a hoot when I told her that was my middle name. She knew the town I came from and said her husband traveled there sometimes on business. I thought *that* was a hoot. I grew to dearly love Mrs. Myers. She made my stay in reform school bearable. And she did keep her eye out for me.

There were times I would be put on the housekeeping list for the week as a normal part of the rotation and Mrs. Myers would say she really needed me in the laundry that week. This would sometimes get me out of the housekeeping detail until the next rotation. The times she couldn't get me out of it, I would do my best, knowing I would be back in the laundry the following week.

There were times I had to be on the sewing room team as well. I hated that more than housekeeping. It was so boring darning socks all day — not at all my idea of a good time. I was never a person who liked sitting all day long. I liked to be on my feet, moving.

Kitchen duty was one of my regular duties each day. Kitchen girls had to get up at five thirty, half-an-hour earlier than everyone else. I waited for the officer in the girls' dining room most of the time, but there were a few times I had to wait on the officers' dining room. It was huge and was where all the staff and officers ate except for Mrs. Story, who was always too busy in the kitchen.

I hated waiting on the officer in the girls' dining room because she was the same officer who was on the desk upstairs, and who was usually the one on housekeeping. She didn't like me and would always look for ways to push me, like telling me she was just having coffee that morning, then complaining I did not put a plate for toast and a butter knife on the table for her. If I tried to remind her she said she only wanted coffee, she would shut me down like my mother and father always did. I learned to bite my lip with her. I would often feel like it might start bleeding I was biting it so hard.

I loved waitressing for the officers' dining room. I had to learn all the little quirks these people had. Like Mrs. Davis at night only had a cup of hot water instead of coffee or tea with her meal. I learned how to be polite when serving. I learned how to set a proper table. We used all kinds of silverware and I had to learn the proper placement of the forks, spoons, and knives, as well as the serving silverware, what plates went where, and proper placement of glasses and coffee cups.

I loved learning these things. In the laundry room, I learned the right way to iron a shirt. Who would think there was an actual right or wrong way to iron a shirt? Collar, yoke, sleeves, and body. In home economics when I was in high school, the teacher asked that question one day and was surprised I knew the answer.

When I was in housekeeping, I was learning how to clean a bathroom. I learned to wash and wax a floor. I had never before heard of a buffing machine. My mother and sister did all the cleaning in our house. My mother washed and waxed our floors and never showed me how to do it. I don't think I ever cleaned a bathroom. I made my bed at home, but not the way I had to do it there. We had to have hospital corners. I only just turned fourteen and had so many things to learn, but I was like a sponge; I soaked it all up. All the things I was learning would stay with me for my whole life. They were important things that, as a girl, I would need to know when I was an adult.

Sundays were visiting days. The first four weeks after I went back, my grandmother came to see me. She brought my aunt with her a couple of times and brought my mother once or twice. Other than that, I didn't get visitors. When my grandmother visited, she sometimes brought me a couple of dresses she made. I didn't even know she could sew. The dresses were floral print and had lots of orange in them. I think they were orange trees. She also brought me a leather jacket. It was bright orange. I'm sure it was not real leather, but it was attractive. The girls all remarked about the color but I wasn't sure if I liked the color or not. What I did know was my grandmother bought it for me, so I loved it. I'm not sure if I told them it was or not, but all the girls believed my favorite color was orange. Sundays we could wear our own clothes. I always wore one of those dresses and the bright orange jacket with pride to church each Sunday.

One time, when my aunt came to visit with my grandmother, she mentioned something about when Nana gets custody of you. I felt sick to my stomach. I told her I was not going to live with my grandmother. I couldn't explain to them why I couldn't go live with her, but I think it hurt my grandmother and was why she never came back to see me. I know now it was not because I didn't want to, but because I felt like I would be betraying my mother. As much as she hurt me, she was still my mother and I was a loyal person to the core of my soul. Despite everything, I could never betray her.

Not having visitors on Sunday became so routine, I did not want to dress up on Sundays anymore. I just changed into my evening clothes after church. Though not as pretty—actually they were kind of ugly—they were more comfortable than dresses and nylons. They didn't have panty hose back then. You had to wear garter belts with nylons. I was so short that the part of the nylon you put in the garter belt needed to be rolled down to get them to fit, which caused the nylons to sag and to run more easily Even the smallest pair of nylons were huge on me. Who wanted to wear saggy nylons all day? Not me, that's for sure.

Not having company on Sunday meant you had to spend the afternoon in the TV room watching old black and white movies. They might not have been old then. But they were the kind of movies old people liked. I hated sitting there for what seemed like all day. Three hours from one to four were visiting hours. It got to the point where I talked them into locking me in my room for that time. I would rather sleep through the afternoon then be stuck watching old black and white movies. So, each Sunday at one I got locked up until visiting hours were over.

One day, an officer told us they were having an outing. Only four girls could go. The requirement to go was you had to be a person who didn't get visitors and have good grades for the month. Wanda, me, and two others went, but I don't remember who they were. It was held at the John F Kennedy Memorial Coliseum. I don't remember the name of the band that was playing, but I had a blast. It was a great Sunday afternoon. I was grateful I was not in housekeeping that month since we were graded each week by the officers on our chores as well as behavior. I always got good grades on my chores but when it came to behavior, it varied. If I was in housekeeping with the officer who didn't like me, I might not have great marks there. She looked for things to mark me down on. Plus, my mouth would still sometimes override my brain and get me in trouble.

One time, Officer Mrs. Grumpy was covering for another officer who was out sick, so she was working on Saturday. That was the day Catholic girls went to confession in the afternoon and she had to bring us that week. We only had one church. It was used for Protestants and Catholics. Each Saturday after confession I would put a special curtain up for the Protestant service. The Protestants went to church first. The next morning someone would take the curtain down after the service so we Catholics could have our service. The officer was yelling at me about something I was doing and I mouthed off, saying I knew what I was doing better than she did since I did it every week. She was not amused and pulled me right off the altar. When we got back to our building, right in front of it, I told her she was getting reported and she slapped me across the face. The shear shock of her doing that made me cry. I don't remember if I tried to report her or not. I was so happy she usually only worked on weekdays because I could avoid her for the most part during the week. But God forbid if she was there on a Saturday, I was pretty much screwed. I could not avoid her then.

After you were in there for four months, you could have a weekend furlough. It would be from Thursday morning at nine o'clock until Sunday at four o'clock on the last week of the month. My first one was in July. They called my name at nine o'clock sharp. I went down to the office and my mother was there. I don't remember who drove her, since she didn't have a license, but she seemed happy to see me and I was genuinely happy to see her. It felt strange though because I had not seen her since April when she came to visit with my grandmother.

I was thrilled to be going home for four days. One of the stipulations of going on a furlough was I always had to be with a parent the entire time. This meant I had to go to work with her, which was not a problem since she worked at a cab stand as a dispatcher and I could be there. I went to work with her each night and I loved it. The people who drove the cabs talked to me when they were there hanging out. They joked with my mother and bought me sodas and junk food. But most important, my mother and I could talk.

She was not mad at me when I was home. We didn't talk about anything that happened. She told me stories about when I was a baby, how funny I was, how much I would make everybody laugh doing silly stuff, and how I loved the attention I got from being funny. She told me I was afraid of cement and when she took me outside I would grab her arm and pull myself up so my feet would not touch the cement. She said I would not put my feet down until we reached grass and that I did that until I was three years old. She told me she didn't know why I was afraid of it, just that I was. I told her some of the funny stories about things that happened in reform school and told her about my friends there. It was an awesome weekend. My mother got me back to the reform school at four o'clock sharp. Again, I don't remember who drove us.

I hated being back. This was my first furlough, and after a furlough, the girls had to stand in line awaiting an exam to make sure you didn't bring crabs (pubic lice) back with you. I had never heard of them and it was a humiliating process. We kept our dresses on but had to remove our undies and one by one, go into the nurse's office and have our pubic area examined to make sure we didn't have lice. It was a quick process and of that I was glad, but it felt degrading. I was only fourteen and not sexually active. The other girls were sixteen and seventeen. Maybe they were active, but I don't know. We didn't talk of such things.

There were some girls who were pregnant. Other than eating with us, the pregnant girls were kept separate from us. I used to feel bad for them, unable to imagine what it must be like for them to be stuck in this place while having a baby. Some were going to have their babies and go home with them. Others were planning on giving them away. I remember one girl who planned to give her baby away changed her mind when she had her baby. I was told she decided to keep him, and was happy when I heard that.

My next furlough came, and I waited to hear my name called. It never was. Lunch came and went with no mother. I spent the day in the laundry ironing. The other girls said I should not do anything since it was my furlough day, but I didn't mind ironing. I liked it. Also I had to do something to keep busy. I felt like I was dying inside. Every hour that passed, I died a little more. By supper time I could not hold the tears back. I cried for the rest of the evening. I cried so much they called the psychiatrist in to talk to me.

He asked me all kinds of questions about why my mother might not have picked me up. Did I do something wrong when I was home last time? No, I didn't do a thing. My mother and I did not have one problem the whole time. I told him I thought she just didn't love me. I thought she decided she didn't want me anymore. Mrs. Davis let me call my mother earlier in the day, but she would not talk to me. My sister answered and said she had no ride there. I know Mrs. Davis called my mother as well.

I can honestly say I was completely devastated. In my entire life, I never before felt that much hurt inside. It was so deep, beyond anything I ever experienced. I felt totally abandoned. I cried for hours on end. I even cried myself to sleep that night.

Around three o'clock in the morning, the night officer woke me. She told me to get dressed, that my mother was waiting downstairs to take me home for the weekend. I remember who brought her to get me this time. It was her boss. She told me she could not get there earlier because she had no ride, but I was so happy she was here, I didn't care anymore about earlier feelings.

For many years, well into my adulthood, I could never bring myself to even think about that day. Trying just brought back so much pain. Mother told me she had to fight with them to get them to let me go in the middle of the night. I never believed her, but thinking about it now, I realize she might have been telling me the truth.

I always believed they had to put pressure on her to pick me up. I don't think they knew what they were going to do with me if she didn't. The pain was unbearable then and as I write this, I didn't realize how painful it would be to me to put it on paper. I've shed many tears in the process of writing this.

I've forgiven my mother for not being able to understand how her actions would impact me. I can say that though she made many excuses about so many things for so many years, deep in my heart, I felt there was no excuse for what happened. None. Unless she was dead, there was nothing that made it okay that she didn't pick me up that day.

I've always believed it, and so many other things, were just a matter of priority and I was not the priority. It is as simple as that to me. My mother worked at a cab stand! The people there who drove were caring people. She had friends who I believed would have brought her. All she had to do was ask, but she did not until forced.

Then there was the question of where my father was during all this. Probably deep in his bottle, not wanting to feel or deal. I only saw him one time while on furlough, in the middle of the night. He came home drunk, as usual, but he didn't fight that night. He just sat and told jokes and we all laughed. Wasn't he the funny one? Everyone around him hurt, but he was a jolly good fellow. That is what addiction does. Addicts create pain for all the people who love and need them. Please don't misunderstand. I realize addicts are in their own personal, private hells as well. Addictions are like the most violent storms—they destroy everything in their path, including the addicts.

Eleven

I learned a lot in reform school and not just about cleaning and stuff. I learned I did not ever want to do drugs. There were addicts there who were so messed up from the drugs it was sad. I didn't ever want to be like that. I never wanted a repeat of what I experienced when I broke my arm, or what happened to me at Becky's. It had taught me I did not want *anything* that would make me unable to protect myself or to ever be out of control of my wits.

I had another experience there that scared me. I had one of my bad stomachaches, and it was so bad, they called in the doctor. He gave me two pills to take. I took them and went to bed. In the morning, they woke me for kitchen duty. I remember being in the bathroom at the sink and telling the person next to me that I was sick. Then I passed out. The next thing I remember was the night officer and a couple of girls trying to help me walk down the hall to my room as I faded in and out of consciousness. They were having a hard time keeping me walking straight. That's all I remember until I woke up in the afternoon.

The experience terrified me. I thought it must have been caused by the pills the doctor gave me. I never learned what the pills were and have always been afraid of any kind of medicine unless I know for sure I have had it before with no reactions.

Other things terrified me in reform school, too. Things I found out about myself. I learned that though I was not usually a follower, I could be talked into stuff I really didn't want to do. One time, some girls decided we were all going to cut our arms with big bobby pins and I went along with them. I had been a razor blade cutter before I came here, but didn't realize there is a big difference between razor blade cutting and bobby pins. Bobby pins hurt a lot and covered a large area when you scrape with them, but I said I would, so I did. I scraped up a whole arm.

We got in a big trouble for that stunt. They made us all have penicillin shots, saying we needed it to make sure we didn't get an infection. I hated needles, so I knew I would not do that again. Also, one night a bunch of the girls said we should bang on doors after we got locked in that night. I agreed I would bang on my door with the rest of them. Lights went out and I heard the first door banged on. I kicked mine a few times then got into bed and went to sleep. I was sleeping like a rock when the lights came on. There, in my room, stood an officer with the same gentlemen who had been in my room after the fire Darlene and Wanda started. They thought I was not really sleeping. Apparently, some other girls took the banging on the door to another level. They broke stuff in their rooms, like things they made in ceramics, shampoo, and other stuff.

I only kicked my door a couple of times, but they considered me one of the ring leaders. They could think what they wanted, but whatever happened wasn't my idea. I didn't think about ways to get into trouble and never went looking for it. I never had to. Trouble usually found me, not the other way around.

There was a huge meeting the next day in the TV room. All the girls were there. Attending were the gentlemen who had been in my room, the head of the house, and some other officers. They were mad at us, but we didn't end up in trouble for some reason. They asked us what we were upset about. We told them things like how inconsistent the officers were. One officer would allow us to sit in our doorway and chat with the girl across the hall while others would punish us for any communication. We told them we knew that every night, the boys in other buildings were allowed to have the fruit and stuff their families gave them on Sundays, while we were only allowed to have it on Tuesdays and Saturdays. We told them that by the time we were able to enjoy what they brought in, it was spoiled.

All that didn't really affect me since I didn't get company, but they changed the rule so we could have it nightly like the boys. We were also allowed to sit in our doorways while in our rooms and chat with the girl across the hall. That was nice because before, when we were in our rooms, we had to be quiet. I was surprised not one person got in trouble as a result of that night. It could have gone badly for everyone, me included. I only kicked my door a couple of times, and it was not my idea, but I agreed to be a part of it and had no idea others would take it as far as they did. Learning I could be talked into stuff made me realize I needed to start thinking about what I was asked to do before I agreed to do it.

* * *

There were some things I loved in reform school. They kept us quite busy. We were either working or in gym or swimming during the day. Nights we would be in the TV room or craft room after dinner until bed. There was swimming Monday, Wednesday, and Friday afternoons. We would all stand by the desk in the hallway after lunch waiting to hear if we were on the list for that day. Loving swimming as I did, I always wanted to go every day, and waited anxiously, hoping my name would be called because usually, you only got to go two of the days.

Some of the girls never wanted to go and would do anything to get out of it, which seemed strange to me. I never before knew anyone who didn't like swimming. Occasionally, if I had been swimming on Monday, and Wednesday, if someone could or would not go on Friday I would get lucky and take their place. I loved those days.

We also had gym on Tuesday and Thursday. Participation

was mandatory. It was where I learned to play softball. I loved that activity and for the most part, was reasonably good at it.

I remember we had a huge field day sponsored by Saint Anselm's, one of the colleges in the area. We had a cookout for lunch and supper that day. I love cookouts. There's nothing like grilled hamburgers and hot dogs. There was so much food that day, including chips, soda, and my favorite—watermelon. It was a blast; a fun-filled, all-day event that ended with an award ceremony with trophies. There were six first place trophies and two for second place. I was so excited for the girls who were getting one. Everyone could pretty much guess who the winners would be just by knowing how the races and games went that day. Certain kids were athletic, others weren't. I was athletic, but was so much smaller, the other girls had longer legs which made it hard beating them in things like racing. But I did my best in every event, which got me points. Though I was not always first I would often come in second or third. I even placed in the pie eating contest, which was a miracle since we had to eat a whole pie. I didn't like pie. Worse, it was a blueberry and I didn't like blueberries. But I was a person who always did my best, so it didn't matter if I liked it or not, I had to try my hardest. Thinking about it now makes me laugh, but I have never eaten a piece of blueberry pie since then.

I must have accumulated a lot of points without realizing it because it was a huge shock to me when my name was called for a first-place trophy. I didn't have a clue I would win one. As I walked up to get it, I could hear everyone yelling, "Yah Peewee" and such. They were happy for me. I was not used to people caring about me and it made me feel wonderful inside, like a million bucks, to hear them cheering for me.

* * *

In June, Becky ended up in Reform School with me for thirty days. I remember how excited I was to hear there was a girl named Becky here from Dover who said she knew me. I was sure it was my bestie. I was in the laundry that day, so I had to wait until after lunch to try to sneak a peek while waiting for the swimming list to be read. I looked in the security window and sure enough it was her. I would like to say I felt bad she was there, and a part of me did feel bad, but another part of me was so happy to see her, the happy feelings won that day and I relished them. I didn't have many happy feelings in my life. I don't remember why she said she was sent there, and because she was only there for thirty days, I didn't get to see her much. She was in housekeeping with Mrs. Grumpy while I was in the laundry. Looking back, I don't remember much about her stay other than the day I learned she was there.

* * *

Earlier, I said I intended to learn to make a sweater. Well I did, and the woman who taught us to knit took them to a fair. I got a blue ribbon. I also got a blue ribbon for a sewing project I did. I made a five-piece outfit. I was learning a lot there.

By this time, my sentence was almost up. I was due to go home in a week, but that didn't happen because one gym day, six of us were not doing what we were told by the coach. We were fooling around and not being serious, and even told Coach we were not going to listen and he was getting angry. Then the joking around took on a life of its own. He would say something and we just kept saying no until he got so mad he called for an officer to take us in. The next thing I knew, we were called before the Discipline Board. Four of us, including Wanda and me, who were not his "pets," were locked up in Security for a week. The other two were locked in their rooms for two days. They were girls who came back to Reform School the same week I did and were in security with me in January.

We all had time added to our sentences. The four who had been locked in security for a week got an extra thirty days. Those who were locked in their rooms got two extra weeks. It was not fair, since we all did the same thing. Also, I think they went way too far for our childish prank. Being locked up for a week should have been enough. It was awful having to stay there a month longer. And being locked up for an entire week was hard, though they did let me bring a deck of cards in the room with me. I played solitaire until I could not stand it anymore.

Wanda was right next door to me, so we talked through the wall. She taught me a game she called cover up. You put two rows of cards four across, then you cover any two that match until all cards are gone. It gave me something to do other than solitaire, so I was happy for that. The only time we got out of the room was to use the rest room. It was a hard week to get through and I prayed a lot. I felt like I would lose my mind at times. Wanda and I would talk when we could, but that was only when the officer was not around to hear us. Other than the cards, there was nothing to do.

My punishment never made sense to me. All we did was to stand still and be a little mouthy when the coach told us to do jumping jacks. I got in less trouble for punching someone! It didn't make any sense.

The month of October seemed to be the longest of the year. I thought it would never end. My new going home date was scheduled for the second week in November and I was anxious for it to come. My time was almost done.

When November arrived, I could hardly believe it. On November 12, 1968 I would be going to my parole hearing. That would determine if I was going home or not. If I passed the parole board I would get to leave right after. I had been doing my best to stay out of any trouble since being locked up and the day before the hearing was no different. I was excited, hardly believing I could be going home the next day. Unfortunately, I ended up in housekeeping that day.

I dusted one of the hallway baseboards and then the girl ran the buffer down the hall right after I finished. The officer said I didn't dust the hall and when I told her what happened, she said I had to repeat it. As I walked away, I muttered "bitch" under my breath. The officer asked me what I muttered. I looked at her but said nothing. The girl with the buffer told her I called her a bitch. The officer was so mad she grabbed me by the arm, opened an empty security room, told me to kick my shoes off, and get in there. Somehow, I managed to have a big bobby pin in the room with me. I am not sure how I got it. Either I brought it in with me or someone slipped it under the door for me. At any rate I had one and I wanted to carve my arms up but knew that would not help the situation. It would likely just get me more extra time. I carved hate and other things under the bed into the floor. I was terrified I was going to get extra time for getting locked up. It was one of the worst days for me.

I was still locked up the morning of my parole hearing. I didn't sleep much that night. I was too busy praying I would be able to go home the next day. I knew if the officer had her way, I would be staying. She was the one I butted heads with the whole time I was there; the one who pulled me off the altar and slapped my face. She hated me and I hated her more. She was the only officer I ever managed to get into trouble with, other than that one time with coach.

In the morning, they let me dress in my own clothes for the hearing. It started snowing as we walked to the hearing. Wanda, I, and a couple of other girls were going to the hearing. When I saw Wanda, she told me she got locked up the day before, right after I did, but she didn't say why. The officer was clearly being a jerk, doing that to us the day before our hearing. Wanda was as afraid as I was.

Each of us would have our own hearing. We were led into a long hallway to wait for our turn. Someone gave us small medals, like a Saint Jude's. I received two of them and held one in each hand while I waited and prayed.

Dr. Yellow came down the hall and passed us. On his way back to the room he looked at us and said, "I hear two of you were locked up yesterday."

Wanda and I both answered, "Yes, sir."

He said, "I guess you better pray then."

I opened my hands, showed him the medals, and said, "I am praying, sir."

He went down the hall and disappeared into the room. I prayed the two hours or so I was in that hall.

I was the last one called into the room. There were three women and two men in there. The only one I knew was Dr. Yellow. He was the director of the State Industrial School. He was one of the gentlemen who were in my room on two occasions — once when Darlene and Wanda started the fire and again the night right after what they called a riot, where I kicked my door a few times and went to sleep.

I was terrified. I had no idea what to expect. I was asked a lot of questions. If they allowed me to go home, what would I do if this happened or that happened. I answered them as best I could with what I believed they wanted to hear.

One question was, "What if your mother says you can do something you know you're not allowed to do, like hang out with another girl who has been in here?"

I said I would not do it even if she said it was okay. I told them I would follow the rules they set for me.

They asked what I would do if I was having problems with my mother. I said if I was having any problems, I would tell my parole officer when she visited me. I was still only fourteen years old and would be on parole and have meetings once a month for the next two-plus years, until I was seventeen.

I knew when I went home I would do my best to follow all the rules. I knew that meant I could not hang around Wanda even though she was going to a foster home in my town. It also meant hanging around with Becky or Debbie would not be permitted, but I didn't care. All I wanted was to go home.

After the hearing, we were driven back to the girls building around lunch time and the waiting began. It was not until around supper time we were told the Parole Board ruled we could all go home. There was so much excitement when we heard the news. We could hardly believe we were going home. It was exciting but scary at the same time.

It was still snowing outside. What started as a few flakes earlier in the day was now a raging storm. When they called my mother, she told them she had no way to come get me due to the storm. I was devastated when they told me and I broke down. Wanda was going into a Foster Home in Dover.

Thankfully, a woman who was a volunteer at the reform school was a daughter in the family Wanda was going to live with. She offered to drive me home when she heard my mother was not able to pick me up. She talked to Mrs. Davis who phoned Dr. Yellow and they agreed to let me leave with her and Wanda. Thank God it was a day she was there volunteering. It was my lucky day after all. I made it through the hearing and had a ride home.

Wanda and I left the State Industrial School right after supper the evening of November 12, 1968. When I learned I was leaving with Wanda, I was so excited I packed my stuff as fast as I could.

They allowed us to say goodbye to the other girls. I never expected to, but I cried my eyes out. I had a lump in my throat, like when my aunt dropped me at home one time when I was a little girl. Most of these girls became my friends. I just spent almost nine months with them, from March 27th until November 12th. Though they became an integral part of my life, I knew I would never see them again. Other than our daily assignments, we did everything together and I came to love those girls. I have thought about them many times over the years and can see their faces when I think about them. I wish I could see some of them again so I can ask how their lives have been. I hope life has been kind to them. Living together in that place created a bond we all shared and I hope they remember me with the same fondness I remember them.

* * *

The woman driving us home was very nice. I knew her from her volunteering. I will never forget she stopped at the first store we came to and asked Wanda and I if we wanted anything. We asked for the same thing Debbie and I had asked for – Winston cigarettes and a Pepsi. She got them for us, and we smoked to our hearts content all the way to Dover.

I don't remember much about arriving home. I know it was late when I was dropped off, but can't remember if my mother was there or at work. It felt awkward being home after being gone for so long. I never told anyone, but though I was glad to be out of reform school, I was also afraid. I think I cried myself to sleep that first night home. I can't explain why. It was probably just a whirlwind of emotions about all that transpired over that last year.

Reform School had been a haven for me. I was there at the most volatile time in my life. So many things happened to me before I went there, and my young mind was not able to understand or cope with it all. Worse, there was nobody to turn to for help and I could no longer even trust myself since I was cutting my arms all the time. I hated myself more than anyone else. Things in my home were so explosive, I no longer felt safe there. I was afraid all the time. I felt totally lost and alone. Nothing mattered to me anymore. The only feelings left inside me were pain, anger, fear, or emptiness. I believe I was beginning to lose the will to live and was writing songs about getting killed.

Reform school helped me by taking me out of it all. It was a refuge, and though I hated being locked up, I felt safe. Nobody was going to hurt me there. It felt safe to take my clothes off. I could take a bath and sleep with a nightgown on instead of my jeans. I felt like I fit in somewhere for the first time in my life. I didn't feel like I was on the outside looking in anymore. I learned I could have fun. I learned to laugh again, something I had not done in a long time. I began to trust others as well as myself again. I didn't carve my arms up when I got locked up the day before the parole hearing, even though I wanted to. That was huge progress for me.

* * *

New International Version - Psalm 91:1-2
Whoever dwells in the shelter of the Most High will rest in the shadow of the Almighty. I will say of the LORD, "He is my refuge and my fortress, my God, in whom I trust."

* * *

A couple of times, we had college girls from Saint Anselm's

come visit us, sort of Big Sisters. Although I was still too ashamed to tell anyone what the boys had done, I did find the courage up to tell one of the girls about my mother and how she hated me and was beating me up. Until that time, I only told Officer McCarley about the one beating. This young woman didn't look down on me or say it was my fault. She had compassion for me, not pity, and it made all the difference to me. This young woman's compassion allowed me to build tiny buds of trust. I was letting out some of the pain I had been living with.

Knowing my mother hated me was very painful, much more painful than her hitting me. I wanted her to love me but no matter what I did, she could not give me the love I needed. It seemed like I was always a disappointment. She was always angry at me. What I finally learned was it was her problem, her failing, not mine. I was a kid; she was the adult. That is not to say I was perfect by any stretch of the imagination. There were times I certainly pushed the limits way beyond what was reasonable, and there were times she had every right to be angry at me, but what I learned was that, although she was mad at me, the way she handled it was wrong. She should have learned how to deal with anger in a healthy way. It was wrong to withhold love from me because she was angry. It was wrong for her to blame me for everything that disappointed and angered her. Her anger and frustration at my father was too often taken out on me.

I was then, and still am, a deeply sensitive and compassionate human being. What my mother didn't know was that I loved her more than life, and it hurt me that my dad didn't treat her the way she deserved. She had no idea how many nights I cried myself to sleep feeling bad because she hurt so much.

* * *

I learned some things about myself in reform school. I learned I was a strong, tough girl, though I was no longer the tough-as-nails girl or the child with the tough outer shell to protect my fragile underbelly. No, the girl I found emerging was strong and tough enough to leave her shell for small periods of time to venture out enough to begin learning a little bit about trust and other things. I learned I deserved respect and had value. I learned I was resilient.

I was beginning to grow up. I was no longer a tomboy. I was becoming a young lady. So much happened since I turned thirteen, but it seemed like a lifetime ago, like it happened to someone else. I suppose in some ways it did. I was not that vulnerable little girl anymore. I was going to be fifteen and didn't feel so alone or afraid anymore.

Age 15

I would love to say things were wonderful with my mother after reform school, but they were not, though I can say they were much better than they had been. She no longer hit me, and we didn't fight like we did in the past. I think we both learned something while I was away. My mother and I always had such a volatile relationship and it was nice not to be fighting all the time. Though I can't say I felt an overwhelming amount of love from her, at least the hate seemed to be gone.

I could tell she still didn't really like me, but had gained a certain amount of tolerance. My father continued to drink, and he and my mother fought less, but she was still in a lot of pain due to his behavior. One night I woke to find my mother standing over me, bleeding. I am not sure if what woke me was the blood dripping on me or her yelling that it was all my fault. She had a razor blade in her hand and had cut her wrists. She kept saying look what you made me do. I gathered from what she was saying that it was my fault because I taught her about razor blades by cutting my arms.

I jumped up and grabbed her by her arms screaming for my

sister to come take the razor blade away from her and call 911. Karen took the blade away while Linda called. The police came and took my mother to the hospital. A few hours later, she came home with her wrists wrapped up. I always wondered if I forgot a fight she and I had earlier that night. I just know what she did and what she said.

When Mother got home, nothing was said about what happened. Everyone just went to bed. That's how it was in our house. Things were never talked about. We were all just left with our feelings locked inside ourselves. To this day, that night has never been discussed by my sisters and me, though it did leave scars on my heart.

My mother and I did talk about that night many years later. When I asked her why she woke me up the way she did, all she could say was she woke me because she knew I would help her and was strong enough to stop her from finishing what she was doing. She did tell me it was not my fault, that she cut her wrists that night because she was mad at my father. I don't remember if she apologized to me or not.

Once, we talked about reform school. She said it bothered her I went there and she felt guilty. I told her not to feel guilty because the problems with her were just some of the things going on with me at that time. I told her going to reform school turned out to be the best thing in the world for me, I was glad I was sent there, and she should let go of the guilt. It was what needed to happen at the time and I did not blame her.

We talked about the rapes. She admitted I told her what happened with Rusty and Crooked Teeth. She said that at the time, she just could not believe that something like that really happened, so she went into denial.

I found out Rusty's mother knew as well. One day when I was visiting, she told me Rusty told her about it when she told him Crooked Teeth had been convicted of rape and was in prison. Apparently Rusty told her he was not surprised since his first sexual experience was rape. He told her Crooked Teeth raped me when I was thirteen. I am not sure he told her his role in it, but at least he told her something. She didn't indicate that she knew Rusty's part, and I didn't tell her. I saw no sense in hurting her.

Another time, I was at her house when Rusty called. She said he wanted to talk to me sometime and asked if she could give him my number. I said yes, I wanted to talk with him as well. I wanted to ask him about that day in my cellar when I was just thirteen. It haunted me over the years. Though I long since forgave them, I felt stuck. I wanted to know if my recollection of events that day was accurate. Did it really happen or was it just a bad dream I had? I needed to know.

The next afternoon, Rusty called my house. It felt like a call I had been waiting a lifetime to receive. I asked him to please be honest with me. I straight up told him what I remembered about being raped, then asked if my memories were correct. He told me it did indeed happen and admitted he had helped Crooked Teeth that day. He didn't offer an explanation, nor did I ask for one. I don't remember anything else that was said other than he was coming home in a week or so and would like to meet me and talk. It was not a long phone call and when I hung up the phone I just stood there stunned, unsure if I said yes or no about meeting him when he came home.

I was glad he was honest, but admit it shocked me. Our conversation that day lifted a weight I carried since the rape. I knew I could completely let go of it now. His being honest about what happened set me free and relieved much of the guilt I felt about it. I was feeling a little bit lighter. I never did get another call from him.

He did come home, but it was in a body bag about two weeks after our phone call. I think he had a heart attack, but I'm not sure. There are times I still think about the day he called, and thank God he had the guts to be honest. He gave me back a part of myself. I don't remember if I told him I forgave him, but I think he knew. At least I hope he did.

Twelve

The process of healing was not an instant or even relatively quick or easy process. It has been the work of a lifetime. I had to learn to take control of myself, and to find a way to love the child within me who felt so unlovable—to love myself.

I always believed I should not have been born, and that the world would be better off if I had not. Throughout my life, I felt like I was always apologizing for my very existence, even as I was learning I had a right to be me, a person who had value, who mattered. Over time, with much work, I stopped apologizing for just being.

God created me, therefore he loved me, and I had a right to be here. God has been very patient with me. He builds me up on the days I feel like I don't matter, and on the days I feel I don't deserve to have anybody care about me, I remember He loves me.

* * *

New International Version - Psalm 139:13-14
For you created my inmost being; you knit me together in my mother's womb.
I praise you because I am fearfully and wonderfully made; your works are wonderful, I know that full well.

* * *

When I got out of Reform School, I went to the Junior High. My study hall teacher, Mr. Gabor, asked me one day if I would like to go to dinner with him and his wife Gloria to a special event. I think he could tell I felt afraid. He assured me his wife Gloria would be with us the entire time and that they would need to meet my mother. I don't know what made me say ok, but I did. Mr. Gabor and his wife Gloria met me at the cab stand where my mother worked. I instantly felt at ease with his wife. She was a lovely woman, a true lady.

We went to something called Businessman's Fellowship. We had dinner at this event, and the speakers were young people who had been addicted to drugs and now lived in a halfway house of some sort. They talked about how they were freed from their addictions through Christ. They said it was his love which freed them when nothing else did. They said, Christ saved them and changed their lives because he loved them. I don't remember the exact words they used, but I could tell they were speaking from their hearts and was completely in awe. I remember thinking and feeling *I* needed this Christ they were speaking about and needed his love, too, but I said nothing to the teacher or his wife.

On the way home, Gloria asked if I would like to go to church with them on Sunday morning. If so, they would be glad to pick me up. Again, I have no idea why I said I would like that, but I did, and on Sunday, they picked me up and I went to church with them. My memory of it isn't clear, but it was either that Sunday morning or the next I told them I wanted to have Jesus as my Savior. I was told about how much God loved us. They said I needed to understand I was a sinner. I had no problem with that as I knew with every fiber of my being I was a sinner and needed saving

* * *

King James Bible - Romans 3:23
For all have sinned, and come short of the glory of God;

King James Bible - Romans 5:8
But God commendeth his love toward us, in that, while we were yet sinners, Christ died for us.

King James Bible - John 3:16
For God so loved the world, that he gave his only begotten Son, that whosoever believeth in him should not perish, but have everlasting life.

* * *

The things I heard about Jesus were some of the things I heard in the Catholic Church growing up, but somehow it all seemed more real than when I was young. I started going to church on Sundays with the Gabors and their three children. They picked me up in the morning and I would spend the day with them. Then we all went to Sunday evening service. It was my favorite day of the week. I lived for Sundays. I could feel how deeply they cared about me and I loved them as well. They will never know how much they mattered to me. I still feel sad I eventually lost touch with them.

I was dating a guy, Jack, who would become my husband. He was jealous of the time I spent with the Gabors and set out to tear me away from them and the church. He pressured me to not go to church, and there were some things going on in the church that I was concerned about, so I eventually backed away from it. He told me he didn't like me going to church because I spent the whole day on Sunday with the Gabors and he wanted me to spend the day with him.

Jack and I met at the Midnight Hour when I was thirteen, about a week before the assault that happened in November. Karen was dating his younger brother, Jerry. They had asked me to dance with him, so as a favor to them, I said ok. We danced a couple of times that night. He was seventeen and I was thirteen and didn't like boys at all. He called me a few times and we talked, but that was the extent of our relationship until I was fifteen.

Just before I turned fifteen, my mother let me go to the

movies a couple of times with him, Karen, and his brother. Once I turned fifteen I was allowed to date him and he became my best friend for a long time.

I had already met the Gabors and was regularly going to church with them. After a few months of dating, he convinced me he wanted to go to church as well, so he and his cousin Danny started attending for a little while on Sunday nights. I am not sure how many times he came, but eventually he went to the front of the church to accept Christ as his Savior. At the time, I believed he was sincere in his desire to have Christ in his life, but years later, he told me he only came to find a way to get me to stop going. We were married for a few years when he told me that. I still remember how betrayed I felt. His influence on me was a contributing factor, but not the only reason why I stopped going to church. There were also things I found confusing going on. Many people were not getting along and others left the church, which also contributed to my leaving.

Once I stopped attending church, I no longer saw the Gabors and eventually lost touch with them. I have not seen them since I was sixteen. I did not invite them to my wedding because I felt ashamed about getting married at only seventeen. I figured they would not approve, so I didn't tell them. That is one of the biggest regrets of my life. I think about them at times and wish I could tell them how sorry I am, and how much of an impact they made on my life. It was because of them I was able to turn my life to Christ. That was the greatest gift they gave me. I needed his love and theirs at that time in my life and I will always be indebted to them. Someday, I hope to see them again in heaven.

* * *

After marrying Jack in 1971, I had two children, a boy in 1973, and a girl in 1976. My children are both grown and live in the same town I do. My son lives with a woman and has three daughters. One is twenty-six, another twenty, and another just turned fourteen. My daughter is married to a wonderful man.

They have two sons, one thirteen and one eleven. My daughter spends her days working with her husband in his business and taking care of my grandsons. She is a devoted mother who adores her boys.

Unfortunately, my marriage to their father didn't work out. We divorced in 1978. It was hard for me to admit defeat in my marriage. I loved him and wanted our marriage to work, but it

My sister Karen, my father, and me on my wedding day, age 17

became evident to me over a few years that he didn't love me. He fell in love with a woman he worked with.

After living in a loveless marriage for a few years, I found myself unable to cope and began drinking, and though part of me still loved my husband, I ended up having an affair. I hated myself for it and, of course, neither the drinking nor the affair cured my loneliness. They only made it worse. I eventually stopped drinking and started going to counseling because I knew I needed help. It took a couple of years of counseling and some serious contemplation before I realized there was nothing I could do to fix my marriage. When I finally divorced Jack, it was one of the hardest things I ever had to do.

After we divorced, I tried to pick up the pieces of my life. I was working and trying to raise my children alone. I didn't go out much, but once a week took my son roller-skating. It was still one of my favorite things to do. While we were skating one night, I ran into John, a guy I knew from my past roller-skating days. He was nice, and we began seeing each other and married in October, 1979. I didn't realize when I married him that he was a severe alcoholic and also very abusive. He hid both very well until we said, "I do." Then I quickly found myself in the same place I saw my mother in when I was a child.

I was not like my mother though. I would yell back, which only made things worse. To try to cope, I started drinking on the weekends my children were at their father's house. Of course, drinking didn't help anything, so I stopped again. I started going to church, hoping to find help and peace there, but I found it hard to make friends because I didn't want people to know what was going on in my home. I was embarrassed by how John treated me. He was nasty to me all the time and I felt beaten down to the point where I didn't believe I had any value. I was severely depressed, crying a lot, and didn't know where to turn for help. I felt like a complete failure. The only family I had in the area was a sister and I didn't see much of her because she was struggling with her own life.

I was sure life with my husband could not be much worse until I began to notice how he leered at my children at the dinner table, as if he was waiting for one of them to do something so he could yell at them. Then he began to pick on my children all the time, especially my daughter, and it soon became apparent he hated her, though I could not understand why. She was just a sweet little girl. He began to pick on her every chance he could. I was fighting with him constantly to leave my children alone. He might get away with picking on me, but thinking he could do the same to my children was a BIG MISTAKE.

One night, we were visiting a friend, and my son and daughter were playing in the living room. I was in the bathroom when my son started yelling about his sister pushing him off the couch or something. I'm not sure exactly what happened, but my husband went into the living room to deal with it. He spanked my daughter while she was trying to tell him her brother told her to push him. I could hear my daughter screaming. My husband came into the kitchen as I came out of the bathroom and I went to the living room to see what had happened. My daughter told me the whole story, how she was trying to tell John what happened, but he would not listen and spanked her. She was sobbing like I had never before seen her do. It broke my heart and something inside me snapped.

I walked back into the kitchen, looked my drunken husband straight in the eye, and said, "If you ever put a finger on either one of my children again I will put a knife in your back. I promise you." I could hear myself speaking but it was like someone else saying it. That scared the heck out of me because I knew to the core of my soul I meant every word. That night was the beginning of the end of my marriage to John. He could beat me down, but I would never allow him to beat down my children. After that night I realized I needed to get him out of my life. I knew I needed to divorce him before one of us literally killed the other. John and I were married just three years.

* * *

I started drinking again after my divorce from John. I had a lot of anxiety and found alcohol would take the edge off, so, I drank daily to deal with it, not realizing I was becoming addicted to the alcohol. I didn't date for almost two years, until I met Rob. He was a helicopter pilot, had been to Viet Nam, was in the Air National Guard, and was very nice, a pleasant change from my previous relationships. He lived in Maine, about an hour from where I lived in New Hampshire. We dated for a couple of years, but he worked second shift and had to be in Bangor two weekends a month, so we only saw each other every other weekend. He didn't really have time for a real relationship, so we ended up breaking up, but we remain friends to this day. He was, and is, the kindest man I have ever known.

After that last breakup, I realized I had a problem with

alcohol. I found the amount of alcohol I was consuming was no longer taking the edge off my anxiety and some nights, after my children went to bed, I was drinking more and more, which concerned me.

In April of 1986, at the age of thirty-two, I knew I had to get help with my drinking. I went into a twelve-step program, which is where I learned about alcohol and its effects on me. I put the alcohol down rather easily, but dealing with all the emotions inside me, emotions I spent many years running away from, was another matter.

I watched others come into the program, and their lives seemed to be transformed almost from the minute they stopped drinking, but it was not that way for me. It was as though I was emotionally back to the same desperate place I was in before I went to Reform School. The only feelings I had were hurt and anger. Of course, I had a lot to feel hurt and angry about; a lifetime of it, beginning with my childhood, and piles of crap from two failed marriages and never dealing with any of it.

I was full of anger and resentment and everyone could see it, everyone but me. I justified all my feelings. Didn't I have a right to be angry? After all that happened to me, I believed I did. It would take many more years before I learned my biggest problem was *not* the things that happened to me. My biggest problem was not knowing how to deal with it all, and then let it go. I was so full of anger and bitterness there was no room for anything else. Anger seeped out of my very pores.

People in the program often referred to me as Angry Patty. It was difficult for me to watch others find happiness and wonder why I could not sustain it for any length of time. People in the program would talk about having lots of friends now and I would feel so hurt that I didn't have many. I did not yet understand people didn't want to hang around me because I was so toxic.

The only thing keeping me sober back then was hope. I hoped I would find the peace I saw in others. People would often say to me, "Don't leave before the miracle happens." That was my hope. I took it to heart and hung onto it for dear life. It was all I had.

At this point in my life, I was feeling extremely low. I was dating a guy who was also in the program. He was brand new and I should have known better than to date a newly sober person. There were many red flags telling me to run when I met Roger, but I was so lonely I didn't pay attention to them. Being newly sober, he was still very selfish. He was also a controlling person and could be emotionally abusive as well.

In 1989, Roger and I had been dating for almost two years when, out of the blue a couple of days after Christmas, he told me he was leaving for Florida on January 3rd to work and might stay down there till April or May. He was not sure of exactly when, but he would be back. He told me he didn't want to break up because he loved me. I was floored when he told me his plans. It seemed to come out of the blue and didn't make sense. He had plenty of work, so why did he need to go to Florida. I admit I was suspicious. I didn't like it that he was leaving so spur-of-the-moment either. And I was having a hard time wrapping my head around the thought of him being gone for such a long time.

He left on January 3rd, 1990. The next day, I ran into some friends of ours at a meeting. They were a couple Roger and I hung around with a lot. The wife told me her husband told her that Roger really went to Florida to try dating other people. She said he didn't want to break up with me unless he met someone else. That was his real reason for leaving. When I got wind of that, it suddenly all made sense. My suspicions were confirmed.

At that point, I was fed up with his bullshit and was going to be done with him. I had no way to let him know our relationship was over, but didn't care. As far as I was concerned it was his problem, not mine. Tough Bananas! I knew I was done which was all that mattered to me. That Friday night, I decided to go out dancing. I met my friend Kitty and her boyfriend Charlie at a dance club in our town.

At the end of the evening, I tried to talk them into coming to my house for a late-night breakfast, something we did lots of times after going out. Kitty said she didn't feel like coming over, so she convinced me to let her friend who had been hanging with us most of the night come over. He was a Major in the Army. I danced with him a few times that evening, and he seemed well behaved. Though I didn't know him very well, I said I would be glad for the company, taking Kitty's word that he was a nice guy. She and Charlie both went to school with this guy and assured me he was trustworthy. He wasn't. I found myself unable to stop him from sexually assaulting me.

Early in the morning of January 6, 1990 I was raped for the third time in my life. But I was not a thirteen-year-old child now. I had no room left inside to put up with any more crap and was no longer afraid to tell anyone. I had no intention on stuffing what just happened to me. I would not carry this secret like I had so many others. I went to my friend Kitty's house and told her what happened and told her I thought I should report him. She agreed I should but when I left her house, I was so filled with terror I initially went home. Unlike when I was thirteen, I locked myself in my bathroom for hours soaking in the bathtub feeling completely numb. It took a few days before I went to the police.

After I went to the police, they arrested the guy. They got me a rape advocate to help me. I was completely devastated by what happened and began having daily nightmares and flashbacks, as if the assault opened Pandora's Box.

All the sexual abuse that happened in my life was constantly flooding my mind. Most days I felt like I was going to lose it. The flashbacks made it difficult to function. It was during this time I had a nightmare about when I was three.

In my nightmare, I was age three and I was trying to tell my mother that a man put my hand of top of his privates, but the words would not come out. I kept trying to tell her, but no words came out. Then I was in the hospital and the doctor was trying to get me to talk. I kept saying, "I want to tell you, but I'm afraid. Someday I will tell you," but nothing came out of my mouth.

I woke up feeling terrified. I could remember every detail of the nightmare and lay there stunned for a long time. I was shaking inside as memories came flooding back. I remembered someone put my hand on their privates when I was only three years old and I remembered who it was that night. I believe that incident, that trauma, was what caused the mysterious speech problem that landed me in the hospital when I was three.

There were many other nightmares to deal with as well as the daily flashbacks. It was as though everything that was buried inside me for so long managed to find its way to the surface. Everything I had pushed out of my mind returned — my babysitter's husband, the boy babysitters, the guy in the gas station, being raped those times at thirteen — it all came flooding back. It felt like I was being crushed beneath a raging tidal wave and was drowning in the pain of it all.

I had never dealt with any of it. I kept it bottled-up deep within my soul for so many years but now, I could not stop it from surging to the surface. I was a wreck; anxious all the time and angry beyond words. I suppose it was this anger that surfaced during meetings, which earned me the name Angry Patty.

I found it almost impossible to deal with the pain. The emotions were too overwhelming. Anger was much more comfortable for me. The rape advocate told me about a counseling group for victims of sexual assault. I was so desperate, I decided to go. I was not at all sure it could help, but the advocate seemed to think it would.

Although I was in the group to deal with all the feelings, I was not ready to touch the pain inside me. I found myself stuck and unable to talk about all the hurt. These were things I never gave voice to, things I, for the most part, never allowed myself to even remember, and I was not ready to face the darkness inside. There is a saying in the program — "You are as sick as your secrets." I was beginning to understand I was sick, though I didn't want to admit it.

I was so ashamed of the things that happened to me, I didn't want anyone to know. I blamed myself, believing it was all my fault. *If* I had listened to my mother and not let them in the cellar; *if* I did not go to the gas station that day; *if* I didn't go into Becky's house that night or knew what to do once I was there; *if* I had not let that jerk come to my house that night to have breakfast. There were so many ifs I blamed myself for.

I secretly wondered if I thought I was drugged that night at Becky's house to cover the shame I felt at being unable to say anything or fight them off. It was like I was just there watching it, though it was me it was happening to. I didn't feel anything at all, physically or emotionally, while it was happening, it was those kinds of thoughts which made me blame myself. I have since learned such thinking is common among sexual abuse victims.

As I learned from reading, it is common for people who have been sexually assaulted to blame themselves. They often question everything, including decisions and reactions, like

• Did I dress too sexy?
• Did I lead him on?
• Did I try hard enough to stop him or escape?
• How could my body betray me by getting aroused?
• Why didn't I report this right away?
• Why can't I get over it?

   The answers are things like

• I didn't feel safe resisting
• I froze and didn't know what to do
• I didn't want to make a scene at the party.

As for fighting back, slapping a small, slightly inebriated guy who is likely to back off is much different from slapping a large, aggressive drunk who might not think twice about punching you into submission. Not fighting back DOES NOT make you complicit. It often makes you smart, but it never means it is your fault, and NEVER means you wanted it to happen.

* * *

My thinking was faulty about so many things — not only about blaming myself for everything that happened, but, because it happened to me at the hands of males, all males were bad. In my mind all men were child molesters, rapists, or at least womanizers. I didn't trust any of them and it was clear to others. A counselor at the rape group looked me straight in the eye and said, "You honestly believe all men are either child molesters, rapists, or womanizers, don't you?" She told me she completely understood why I thought the way I did, then said it was not true, adding she thought it was very sad I believed it with all my heart.

I am a person who thinks about what people say and thought a lot about what she said. That night, I lay in bed awake for a long time thinking about it. Her words cut like a knife and I cried when I realized how truly sad it was, how truly sad *I* was. I was living my life with this horrible core belief about men. I prayed that night and asked God to help me. I was not sure what He could do, but I knew I no longer wanted to hang onto that awful belief about men. I was ready for Him to show me the truth, to shine His light into the darkness in my soul.

* * *

**King James Bible - ** Psalm 18:28
For thou wilt light my candle: the LORD my God will enlighten my darkness.

* * *

It was many years before my prayer about God showing me the truth about men was answered. It was answered by Him allowing me to see women I knew well married to Godly men — men who loved their wives; who would not cheat or ever harm a child in anyway; men like my friends' husbands Scott Young, John Wiswell, Kip Phoenix, and my dear friend Rob. I am grateful for the good men in this world. I know with all my heart they are here.

* * *

Knowing everything I was going through was forcing me to see and understand I needed more help than I was able to get from the rape group or the program. I was stuck so badly and wanted desperately to get unstuck. I went to counseling for years, to a rape group, and to a lot of twelve step meetings, yet I felt so trapped in the ugliness of my bitterness and anger. This kept me so sad. Though I saw some improvement in my life — quick glimpses of happiness and periods of time I would feel content, even joyful — they always passed, and I hated when that happened. I wanted lasting relief for my soul.

Something I still had to deal with was Roger. I had not heard from him since his departure for Florida on January 3rd but suddenly out of the blue he called me on Valentine's Day. I told him I didn't want to talk to him and hung up. When I refused to talk to him, and he decided he should high tail it back home to see what was going on. He showed up on my doorstep two days later.

As you can imagine, I was not thrilled to see him. I was a mess and didn't want to get back into the crap I had been in with him. He was putting pressure on me to stay in the relationship and though I tried to say no, I agreed but told him we needed to talk about all that transpired in his absence.

I told him how, when I found out his true plans about Florida, I broke up with him and went out with my friends. I told him about the assault and how angry I was at him. Part of me blamed him for what happened to me because if he had been here, I would not have been out. He told me he understood and wanted to support me.

It was not long before he reverted to his emotionally abusive self; His Majesty, the baby. Whenever he felt I neglected him, he would pitch a hissy fit. He was always trying to control me. My self-esteem was at an all-time low.

I got a new AA sponsor who told me to pick up a book called *Living on Purpose*. I don't remember the author. There were exercises in the book to help you learn about yourself. One day, I was working on a chapter that asked me to think about what my life would be like **If??** I had to fill in the blank. I found myself thinking so many things could be possible **If** I let go of Roger; **If** I took back control of my life. I began to picture what my life could be like **If** Roger was not in it; **If** I left Roger and focused on myself and my healing. I started to believe the possibility that I could find peace. I felt exhilarated just imagining a different life.

I decided to end my relationship. I told Roger I was breaking up with him, but never imagined what might, or would, happen. He had a volatile temper and went nuts and started to physically threaten me. He had a black belt in karate and I was terrified. I didn't know what to do and believed he might really hurt me, or even kill me. He was so verbally abusive over the last four or five months of our relationship, I was emotionally and psychologically beaten down, probably worse than ever before. I ended up calling a shelter for battered women. That was a hard place for me to find myself. It was difficult to admit I got myself to the point where I was in a shelter and going to meetings for battered women. Emotional abuse is very destructive. I didn't have an ounce of self-esteem left at the end of that relationship. When I was in the shelter, I had to go to yet another kind of meeting; one specifically for battered women. I wrote the following after the first meeting. They published it in their newsletter, but I felt so ashamed being there, I asked them make the author Anonymous. This is what I wrote:

A Beginning
by Anonymous

I woke up this morning, a feeling of sadness lurking
in my soul. I knew things would never be the same.
As I dressed, my thoughts raced across my mind
ever so swiftly. I tried to focus on only one thought.
Pain and anger surged through my heart as the
thoughts drifted away, leaving just one final feeling.
I need to feel safe. I have a right to safety. But how,
where could I find this only God could know. I
certainly couldn't comprehend, hurt was all I felt.

I was urged to go to a support group for victims of domestic abuse. I knew it was a new beginning, but when I got to the group, I sat there feeling alone, not wanting to hear the truth. As I quietly listened to the other women share their stories and feelings, tears streamed down my face, but I couldn't utter a sound. I could only sit and let my tears fall freely as I learned we all shared broken dreams. It seemed to bond us. It was a feeling I never before encountered and it gave me hope. The pain I felt in my heart and in my soul was shared by each member of the group and I knew they knew it, too.

I also wrote this while I was there:

> Broken dreams, now broken denial. I will never be the same. I am not alone. I will not remain a victim. Still my heart is heavy. Tears of sadness fill my eyes, yet, they just sit there. A small reminder that I can, I will, I must transcend. —July 1990

Things in my life had spiraled so far out of control. I was completely desperate. I felt like I could not take much more. I cried myself to sleep each night and continued to have nightmares. I was working hard on myself, but my progress was slow. I was the epitome of sadness and anger. I had no idea how to deal with anything. I felt like I was the walking dead.

One of the things causing me deep pain was that I was supposed to go to court for the assault. When the advocate came to talk to me about the hearing scheduled to begin the next morning it had sent me into the worst night of my life thus far. I started reliving all that had transpired close to a year ago when I had been assaulted. I was so messed up I knew that I could never go to court and speak about all that had happened to a room full of strangers. When the advocate came to pick me up in the morning I told her I could not do it. It was the final blow to my self-esteem.

Not long after, a friend told me about a place called the Caron Foundation. It was an Adult Children of Alcoholics Program. He and his wife went through it and he thought I could find the answers I needed by going there. They told me it was an intense program, but I didn't care. I was desperate for help after the rape the previous year, but it was too difficult to talk about in the rape group. I know now I was not ready at that time to touch the pain inside me, which was the reason all people saw was my anger. I finally came to the realization that I needed to deal with all the anger, and decided to give the Caron Foundation a try.

If I remember correctly, you needed five years sobriety to go there. My sobriety date was April 1986 and I applied to go for January, 1991. I was so close to five years I was accepted.

I was so excited as I flew into Reading, Pennsylvania and traveled to the Foundation campus in Wernersville. I was also afraid because the program was going to be intense. It would take me and my emotions to very dark places in my childhood, a process which would be extremely painful. It was an in-house program and you were there from late Sunday afternoon until mid-morning Friday.

Months before going, I had to fill out a long questionnaire about my childhood as well as about my sobriety and support system. The questionnaire asked very personal questions which helped the counselors tailor a program specifically for individuals.

I was astounded by the program and found the knowledge of the therapists, as well as their ability to implement such individual treatment, amazing.

There was individual as well as group counseling. Each person was assigned things they needed to do; things that depended on your role in your family, as well as the specific things you needed to work on. We were also required to take part in group things. And we each had our own personal thing we were working on for the week.

Since I had been a scapegoat in my family, I was assigned to write down everything I could remember being blamed for. I had to keep paper with me at all times so when I remembered something, I could jot it down. I was surprised how much I was remembering.

The program also educated us about Adult Children of Alcoholics and the different roles children take growing up with dysfunction. I learned so much about my parents, my siblings, and myself while I was there. The way the program was set up made it safe for people to share their deepest pain, which I thought was truly incredible. Never in my entire life did it feel safer to share.

I made up my mind before I went there that I was going for broke, which meant I would not hold back anything. I would put my heart and soul on the line. I would trust them with all my pain, all my feelings, and all my secrets, and trust them to teach me how to deal with my pain and anger. I wanted complete freedom from all the turmoil I carried inside me.

I can't say it was an easy process. I found it very difficult at times to allow myself to feel the feelings, especially those that tended to overwhelm me. And the pain was still more difficult for me to express than the anger. I was still a person who would rather die than cry. I think I was afraid if I started to cry I would never be able to stop. But I knew if I was to get the full benefit of being here, I would have to put my heart on the line. I would have to reach deep below the anger to the very core of my soul.

The anger was like chains holding me hostage; a Band-Aid over a gaping wound. I needed to break free of these chains and get to the place where I was bleeding. Only then could I begin to heal.

I had to allow myself to express all the pain and brokenness I held so deep inside for so many years. I would have to lay my heart bare and it was terrifying for me to do that. There were things I never allowed myself to remember, let alone told anyone else about. But now they needed to be exposed to the light. The rapes I kept buried, the beatings that hurt my heart much more than my body — everything. Everything that for so long took a toll on me would all need to be exhumed. I felt so much pain inside, I cried and cried until I thought I could not cry another tear, then I would cry some more. I wrote this poem about the tears that I had locked away.

Tears

I met a small child battered and worn
It looked like she'd been through a rough raging storm
Her tiny face sad yet no tears could I see
I asked her what happened, and she confided in me
My heart has been broken but tears I can't shed
They are blocked by a dam I have built in my head
She asked me to help her and I started to cry
She reached for my hand and with relief gave a sigh
The dam was now falling her tears were now free
I was crying her tears because this child was me

I learned many things at Caron, and from additional reading since. I learned about the effect alcohol played in my entire life, not just my childhood. I learned about codependence and how it affected my mother. I learned about the roles other family members played in my and my family's dysfunction.

Here are some roles commonly found in dysfunctional families, based on personal experience and reading I've done:

The Responsible Child, also known as *The Hero*

This is the child who seems older than his or her years; the child who often takes over the parenting role; the one who learns to be responsible and as self-sufficient as possible at a young age. This child makes the family look good to outsiders, which often increases the whole family's perception of their self-worth. They are often the straight-A students, the star athletes, and prom queens in later years. The child's accomplishments often allow their parents to believe they are good parents and good people.

Unfortunately, sometimes The Hero grows up to be rigid in their beliefs, desperate for control of everything, including their children. The Hero can also be compulsive and/or very judgmental of themselves and others, though they may hide it well. Heroes are often successful at their jobs or professions and bask in the attention even as they are mostly cut off from their emotions and who they truly are.

Their hidden problems and belief that conforming to often dysfunctional cultural norms makes them right about everything often makes them unable or unwilling to admit there is anything about themselves that is less than optimal, or that might need healing.

The Act-Outer, also known as *The Scapegoat*

This child is often the most honest, especially emotionally, will act out the anger and tension the rest of the family ignores or suppresses, and serves as a distraction from the real and serious issues that face the family. The Scapegoat often has trouble socially and in school because they learn mostly negative ways to get the attention all children crave. It is not unusual for Scapegoat teenage girls to seek attention and acceptance that leads to drug use and/or pregnancy.

Because they are so sensitive and caring, they are often romantics, though cynical and distrustful ones. Still, their self-hatred leads to self-destructive behavior and they are often the first person in a family to face law enforcement and/or some kind of recovery.

The Placater, also known as *The Mascot* or *The Caretaker*

When a child becomes partly or mostly responsible for the emotional, and sometimes the physical well-being of their dysfunctional family, they might become the social director or family clown to divert their siblings' and often their parents' attention away from the pervasive animosity and misery of daily life in the home.

This child will often grow into an adult with low self-worth and loads of guilt who spends his or her life helping others. Unfortunately, they can allow themselves to become so centered on other people they never learn how to satisfy their own wants and needs. They have hearts filled with love for friends and strangers, but little or none for themselves.

The Adjuster, also known as *The Lost Child*

This child often survives by doing their best to be invisible. Often introverts, they often deal with reality by avoiding it, even hiding from it, as does a hermit. They live in their fantasies and daydreams, their TV shows, movies, and books, and outwardly express little in the way of feelings and don't generally get upset in front of others.

The Lost Children often grow into adults with low self-esteem who have difficulty expressing emotions. They may crave intimacy and human connection, but also may be too shy or even terrified of opening themselves to others. They may slowly withdraw and become socially isolated to avoid the possibility of being hurt and keep their hearts and psyches safe.

* * *

Learning about alcohol and dysfunction was invaluable to me. It gave me a different lens through which to view my childhood. I had only seen it from my own perspective, but now I had a fuller view of what was happening within my family as I was growing up. It helped me realize my siblings were just as stuck as I was as a child. They were probably in just as much pain as well. We were all swept up in the current of my dad's alcoholism.

A tool used at Caron to help people see the family structure into which they were born was to create it as a sort of living sculpture. You picked someone in your group to play your father, your mother, yourself, and any older siblings, in my case, my older sister. I watched others in my group when their families were portrayed and found the process amazing.

Then came the day for me to see my family on display. I remember looking at my father standing there with a drink to his lips - his *alcohol.*; my mother holding his arm with his drink up representing her *enabling.* I watched my sister trying to fix the situation through being the helpful *hero.* I also watched the person playing me saying, "No it is not my fault" — the *scape goat* response — as the others pointed to her saying, "You did this. It is all your fault" and other things like that.

It was amazing to see how my family members interacted, as though we were in our own little worlds, none of us able to see the others clearly, each of us doing our own little dance. It was hard and sad to watch. It was so painful to watch I had tears streaming down my face as I backed away from what I was witnessing.

I walked to where I put the papers I had been writing all week. Everything I could remember ever having been blamed for was written on those papers. I picked them up and asked the counselors if I could tear them up. They said I could so I tore up the papers then walked over to the people still standing as my sculpture. I put a pile of the paper at the feet of my father, one at my mother's, and one at my sister's. Those playing my mother and sister picked up the papers, but my father had been secretly instructed not to by a counselor standing behind me. He just looked at the papers I laid there. Then, as he turned his back on them and me, the counselor said to me, "Your father is not going to pick up the papers. What are you going to do?" I remember feeling sad, but said to the counselor, "I don't care if he does or not. It's his burden, not mine. I am not picking it back up."

As if that was not hard enough, now it was time to face my anger and give it expression; time to break the chains and release my soul.

Pillows were set up and I was on my knees behind them. A counselor was on each side of me. They were there for protection. I was handed a bataka bat. (A large, foam aggression-exercise bat.) I was to hit the pillows while saying, "I am angry." I did that repeatedly. I guess I was clenching my teeth in-between yelling and screaming because I remember the counselors telling me a few times to unclench them. I remember saying, "I'm angry" and yelling other stuff, but can't tell you what I said because I have no idea. I was lost in a frenzy of pent up rage. Then, like a switch had been flipped in my brain, there was nothing left of the anger. The tension around my mouth disappeared. I was finished and dropped the bat.

I took a breath, stepped back, and felt complete freedom. I felt happy inside and knew I was finally free from the bondage of my childhood. The anger, and bitterness were replaced with compassion and understanding.

* * *

New International Version - Psalm 107:13-14
Then they cried to the LORD in their trouble, and he saved
them from their distress. He brought them out of darkness, the
utter darkness, and broke away their chains.

* * *

I know God never intended me to be weighed down by my
burdens. He invites us to find rest in him. I have always felt
God brought me to the Caron Foundation to find freedom.

* * *

New International Version Matthew 11:28-30
"Come to me, all you who are weary and burdened, and I will
give you rest. Take my yoke upon you and learn from me, for I
am gentle and humble in heart, and you will find rest for your
souls. For my yoke is easy and my burden is light."

* * *

The person leaving that place was much different than the
one who arrived on Sunday. I had been through so much
emotionally in such a short time, and I felt vulnerable inside,
kind of raw. I was in such a safe place, I completely let my
defenses go. But now I was not sure who I was anymore. I felt
naked without my angry shell around me. As I flew back to
Boston, I felt so alone it was kind of scary.

I understood why people who went to Caron were required
to be in counseling when they left. It was to help with their
transitions back home.

The transition for me was not an easy one. I felt afraid much
of the time. I didn't know how to react to things anymore. Since
I let go of my anger, I didn't know how to deal with things.
Anger had always been my protection and it was going to take
some time for me to build up enough of a defense mechanism
to feel safe.

I found myself unable to handle situations and places I was used to being in. I went back to the meetings that had been regular ones for me, but to my amazement, I now saw things that seemed abusive. Some of the people I knew were so angry. People I was around for years now scared me at times. I noticed things I never did before. I broke down so many barriers at Caron I had little protection left, and really was vulnerable.

I decided I had to find new meetings and I thank God I lived in an area that had many to choose from. I found a few where I was able to feel safe. I also continued counseling for quite a while and eventually, as time went on, I felt less afraid.

I had much to ponder over the next few months. First, I had to find out who I was. I was no longer Angry Patty. In fact, when I went to Caron, I introduced myself as Tricia. I no longer wanted to be attached to the name my family called me. To this day I prefer being called my real name, Patricia, or Tricia, except by my family and friends that I grew up with.

My mother, trying to be respectful one time, called me Tricia, but it was very uncomfortable hearing her call me that. Though I thought it was very sweet of her, I had to ask her to please call me Patty. These days, there very few people who know me as Patty.

* * *

Life moves on day after day, and many things changed over the years, as they always do.

My dad passed away from a sudden heart attack in 1995, which I found incredibly painful. I never had the chance to establish the kind of relationship with my father I wanted, which was sad.

My son got into a bad car crash two months later. He broke his right knee and ankle along with his left arm and required extensive surgery on the ankle and arm. I thank God he didn't have a head injury. It could have been so much worse.

Three months later, my three-year-old granddaughter was living with me and I ended up in a three-year custody battle.

She was my first grandchild, my son's daughter. He and his girlfriend never married and neither of them were in a good place in their lives and were unable to care for her. Taking her away from them was one of the hardest things I ever had to do. She remained with me until she was eighteen.

I was also very sick at that time, dealing with chronic sinus problems. I felt like someone pulled the rug out from under me. These things left me with the realization that *anything* could happen at any time. The knowledge of how little control we have in life threw me into a deep depression for the better part of a year.

Then I decided to go back to church. I knew only God could help me and I desperately needed Him, so, I turned my life back to the God I learned about after Reform School, the very God who loved and protected me by putting me there.

My mother was more willing to allow me into her life after my father's death and I began to rebuild a relationship with her. She and I began to talk about life and other things. My childhood was a huge problem for her. I invested so much in dealing with it, to me it was just history, but to her it represented guilt and shame. Because she was not able to just tell me how she felt, it took time for me to understand that. She was a person who never dealt with feelings straight on, but I thank God for helping me figure it all out because it allowed me to approach her with more compassion. If something from the past came up as we talked, she would become angry, telling me to just let go of it. I found it difficult, but eventually I got her to realize that for me, it truly was just history. Eventually she saw how deeply I loved her and that I harbored no malice toward her or my dad. She came to see I understood much more than she realized about why things happened the way they did.

In the years before she died, we were able to talk freely about our lives when I was growing up, and I believe we both were able to find a measure of peace with our past. I knew she loved me, and she knew I loved her.

I thank God for helping me learn so much in my life. People

sometimes say how wonderful it was that I was able to forgive my mother. I can honestly say, once I learned about alcoholism and its effects on the family, it was never a question of forgiveness for me. I never once thought I needed to forgive my mother. For me, it was about having compassion for another human being, which was easy because God showed me she, like all of us, was just a person trying to get through each day. She had no idea how to deal with the ravages of alcoholism and did the best she could. I think my being able to share my thoughts with her helped her to forgive herself. At least it seemed like it did. I know for sure she saw I did not judge her for what happened.

My Life Now

It has been so many years since my visit to the Caron Foundation and freedom. Twenty-nine to be exact. It is hard to believe how much time has passed.

A year after my time at Caron, I went back to school and got my degree in Early Childhood Education.

Looking back at my life, I so wish I was able to go to the Caron Foundation and college before having children. I would have been much better equipped to be a parent.

Unfortunately, my children were almost grown when I went to Caron. Being raised in an alcoholic home left me with such a broken sense of self and little understanding of children. I had no idea how to set boundaries and limits with anyone, including my children. As a result, I found parenting difficult, especially being a single parent.

I wish I could say I never made any of the mistakes my mother made, but sadly, I did. I was a yeller like she was. Though I didn't see myself as a big hitter, I remember a time I was so frustrated with my daughter,* I slapped her face at least four times, first one cheek then the other. She was around thirteen at the time. There were also a few times I backhanded her in the car, frustrated when she would not stop what I called hounding me.

Certainly, she did not deserve that any more than I deserved my mother losing her temper with me.

Looking back at life and myself, it sometimes feels surreal, and I feel the need to pinch myself. It is hard to believe the woman I am today was once so lost and broken.

Today I live a simple, peaceful life. I am no longer plagued by nightmares and self-hate. It amazes me that I can feel such peace and contentment.

I have five grandchildren who I completely adore. Two of my granddaughters are grown with children of their own. One granddaughter is fourteen. I don't see her often. I have two grandsons who live about four miles from me. My daughter and her husband are fabulous parents. She is completely devoted to her sons. My oldest grandson is thirteen and is an amazing trumpet player. Though he is in eighth grade, he plays at a much higher level, including playing with a big band of adults touring around our area this past summer. I was amazed when I went to one of the concerts. My younger grandson is high-energy. He is eleven, plays hockey, and I am lucky enough to watch him play when his game is close to home.

Through the years, I learned acceptance as well as how to let go. Those were big challenges for me. Accepting my childhood and all that happened came easy for me after Caron, but finding self-acceptance and letting go of my guilt at not being the parent my children deserved or needed has been one of my biggest challenges. I have learned to forgive my broken self and move on. I am just a person with feet of clay living my life as best I can.

I completely believe that everything in my life is exactly the way it is supposed to be at this moment. God is in complete control. He has always had me in the palm of His hand.

* * *

Yesterday's Gone

I look in your eyes and remember the way it used to be
When you were both young children looking up at me
It seems so very long ago we were walking hand in hand
Playing together along the shore building castles in the sand
Many years have passed since then time slipped by so fast
Leaving such bittersweet memories and shadows of the past
So many things I wish I'd said and things I wish I'd done
If only I'd known how to be a mom to my daughter and my son
But yesterday is gone so I must move ahead
Leave behind the guilt and shame and tears my eyes have shed
For I can't change those yesterdays no matter how I try
And I cannot spend eternity feeling pain that makes me cry
So today I'll smile brightly at this day God's given me
I'll make the most of it and be the best that I can be
And I will show my children all the love I couldn't show
When they were just such tiny tots so many years ago
And I will bow before my God upon my bended knee
And thank Him for His endless love He freely gives to me

Afterword

I thought long and hard about writing this book. I know the things I have written about might be difficult to read, especially for family members who might not have realized the things going on in our home. I pray everyone reading this account knows I said what I said because it was the way it was. It was not to cast aspersions on or belittle my parents. They, too, were just people with feet of clay living lives being ravaged by alcoholism as best they could. They each had their own struggles with life and I loved them both.

* * *

New International Version - Psalm 23:4
Even though I walk through the darkest valley, I will fear no evil, for you are with me; your rod and your staff, they comfort me.

King James Bible - Psalm 27:5
For in the time of trouble he shall hide me in his pavilion: in the secret of his tabernacle shall he hide me; he shall set me up upon a rock.

King James Bible - 13:34-35
A new commandment I give unto you, That ye love one another; as I have loved you, that ye also love one another.
By this shall all *men* know that ye are my disciples, if ye have love one to another.

The Caron Foundation

Dear Reader,

In addition to their Drug and Alcohol Rehab facility at 243 Galen Hall Road, Wernersville, PA 19565, the Caron Foundation has Recovery Centers in New York, Philadelphia, Massachusetts, and Washington, DC as well as other facilities in the eastern United States.

If you, or someone you know, may benefit as I did from the help available through The Caron Foundation, more information is available on their website – https://www.caron.org.

Patricia

The DeSalles building, where I stayed
during my time at the Caron Foundation.

Thank You

Dear Reader,

Thank you for reading about my journey from darkness to the light of God. It was not easy for me to write. On the contrary, it was very difficult for me to tell my story, to confront and reveal things I kept secret and/or never spoke openly about while my parents were alive. I cried many tears and prayed many prayers over this last year, asking the Lord for guidance and He helped me realize that by sharing my experience, I would be able to banish the demons that haunted me for so many years and, perhaps, help others find their way back to Him.

What I hope you, the reader, take from this account is that God's light is brighter than any dark place; that He is working for our good even when we are not aware of it, like when I was put into Reform School. And even when we don't understand the challenges and burdens He puts in our paths, that God's love and compassion can bring us through anything, and that we need to do what the Bible says — Love One Another.

If you think my story worthy, please mention it to others who may be interested or who may benefit by learning that no matter how or why one falls, God is always ready to help them rise and conquer their demon, be it alcohol, drugs, or anything else.

Thanks again!

Patricia

Acknowledgements

I would like to thank the people who helped this book become a reality—my friends Melanie Young, Ingrid Phoenix, Sally Von Husen, Jamie Kinsley, Fran Reynolds, and Kip Phoenix.

Jamie—a big thank you for helping me learn MS Word basics.

Fran—thank you for reading for me.

Ingrid and Kip—your friendship and love spur me on.

Sally—thank you for the tireless hours chatting on the phone allowing me to bounce stuff off you.

Melanie—I have no words to convey how I feel. Your love and support over the years goes beyond any expectation. You have been the person I could count on no matter what, including the countless tears that have fallen on your listening ears. You are the one person who has been here throughout. You taught me what love and kindness are. I am thankful for your honesty, even when it hurts. Your acceptance of my frailties goes beyond my human comprehension. Thank you for showing me God's love through your compassion and selflessness. I am amazed by you.

I would also like to thank my church family at Emmanuel for your prayers. A special thanks to Pastor John Tate for your advice concerning my cursing in this book as well as the scripture input at the right moment. Also thank you for your sermons that keep me focused on the truth of God's word.

I also need to thank my sisters Karen and Paula – your support for me writing this book, and your willingness to spur me on, even though many of the topics are as painful for you as they are for me, is priceless. Without you two, I could never have written it. Thank you, Karen, for being willing to help me find healing in our relationship through these last twenty years. I am grateful you are my sister. Paula—thank you for being Moms' ear for me since she passed away. I love you both.

Thank you Drykkr (Joe) for all the times you shared truth and knowledge with me. I am humbled by you. And a special thank you to Tom Cormican for your wisdom and help.

I would also like to mention Annie Dodds whose book, *A Widow's Walk Off-Grid to Self-Reliance,* inspired me. Oliver, thank you for affording me the opportunity to tell my story.

Lastly, I thank God for His love toward me, for finding me when I was a lost, broken soul, and for being the Father and protector, I needed. You are the Rock I stand on.

Patricia

Poems

I'll Ask Why

I'm walking down this weary road right now, my cross held high
 For Christ is beside me every step, He hears my every sigh
When I sometimes try to walk alone, the Cross slips from my hands
 Ashamed I look around to see beside me He still stands
He reaches out to take my hand, then says, "Just follow me"
 And as I walk I wonder why He saved the likes of me
I cannot comprehend His love; I'm just a mortal man
 And why He gave His life for me, I'll never understand
So I'll just walk this narrow road, beside Him I will stay
 Because He loved this wretched soul enough to die one day
And when this road has reached its end and I meet Him in the sky
 I'll thank Him first for loving me and then I'll ask Him why

What Mommies Know

It seems like only yesterday you came into my life
I watched you become a woman and then become a wife
And now I watch you blossom as your baby grows within
So many things I want to say but where do I begin
I guess I'll start by telling you what I need you to know
How special was this gift from God for me to watch you grow
Now soon you'll be a Mommy and know what Mommies know
That precious are their children and how much they love them so

(Written for my Daughter, when she was pregnant with her first baby)

Bottle of Booze

There's a little brown bottle you hold in your hand
I watch you in silence as you try now to stand
The floor won't hold you, it feels just like sand
And just as you're falling, you reach for my hand
I cannot help you, this you must know
I've tried many times, now I must go
Addiction's your love now and I can't compete
This battle is yours, for you to defeat
I pray you find peace and find sober ground
Take care of yourself now, I won't be around

My Gift

I was out in the field when I heard the angles sing
 "Born in the City of David today is Christ, the King"
 So to Bethlehem I came, I traveled very far
I followed three wise men, who followed a bright star
 Each one brought a treasure, a special gift for you
 But I had nothing to give. Oh what could I do?
It distressed me so, I wanted to cry
 Then all of a sudden You caught my eye
When your eyes met mine, at once I could see
 There was but one thing You desired of me
It was all of my love, all pure and true
 So my heart was the gift I gave to You

God Made Mom

He took the sun from the sky for the color of your hair
Then took the fragrance from the rose and let it linger there
He knew that this was just a start
So with the moon's glow, He made your heart
He took the softness of the lambs,
With gentle touch, He made your hands
He took the deep dark sand, to sprinkle in your eyes
Then took His heavenly wisdom, to make you very wise
This woman He made between dusk and dawn
 He said, "I think I'll call her mom."

(*For my mom*)

Memories Stay

Two elephants carved out of wood
A memory from my childhood
A little stool once sat upon
Precious moments we shared will never be gone
I sometimes miss my childhood days
When I'm alone my memory replays
The days I sat upon Nana's knee
She'd sing a nursery rhyme to me
A Band-Aid and cuddle to dry my tears
The sound of her voice would calm my fears
A hug, a kiss, and a smile you see
And a treat in the kitchen just waiting for me
Those days are all gone, but the memories stay
In my mind forever for me to replay

(Written after my Nana died)

Death to Life

Blue skies turned the darkest grey
The day I heard you passed away
Tears poured down, my heart was broke
I could not speak lest I choke
Bowed down low with pain and grief
Suddenly I heard the Savior speak
Dearest Child, look and see
She left your world to be with me
She is not dead, she lives my friend
And you will see her once again
She passed from Life to Death to Life again
Her glorious beginning, not the End

(Written after my Mom's death)

Look To Christ

Little sister, I know you suffer each and every day
I want to help you through this, but I'm not sure what to say
Instead I'll tell you what I know is positively true
God above who sees us all is watching over you
He hears your every whimper, sees your every tear
He listens quite intently to every little prayer
I know He loves you deeply, more than words convey
He can help you through this in His unique and special way
When the pain and anguish is more than you can bear
Jesus Christ your Savior is as close as your next prayer
Remember when you're hurting and don't know what to do
Just reach out to Jesus Christ, He'll reach right back to you

(Written for my late sister Linda when she was suffering with Ovarian Cancer)

Comfort

He knew you in your mother's womb
He knew you from the start
He knows each prayer you keep unspoken deep within your heart
He knows you need His mercy
He knows you need His love
He sent the Holy Spirit, that sweet Celestial Dove
To lift you when you're falling
To cheer and comfort you
When your whole world is shattered and you don't know what to do
Within you prays the Spirit, which none but God can hear
For God to lift your broken heart and calm you from your fear
To Him, to us, you're precious, my dearest Joanie girl
A priceless treasure from the Lord, a bright and shiny pearl

(Written for my late, dear friend Joanie when she was suffering with Breast Cancer)

If Only

If only I could touch one heart
How blessed I would be
If only one person could see your face
By looking right at me
If only my words could reach a soul
Pointing to Jesus who can make them whole
If only my life were not lived in vain
If someone found you Lord through my struggles and pain
If only the peace you Breathed in me
Could bring hope to another that you can set them free

Joy Cometh in the Morning

There is a place way deep inside that only God can fill
For He alone can calm the storm with a whisper peace be still
Way in the depths of each man's soul the darkness seeks the
  light
The unspoken prayers and uncried tears are naked to God's
  sight
It's in that place where shadows fall through darkness and
  despair
That you can meet Him face to face, He waits for you right
  there
He abides within your broken heart to comfort your deepest
  sorrow
To dry the rains from yesterday bring sunshine to tomorrow
You can see Him when the morning breaks beyond the night's
  deep longing
He's the ever-present promise that Joy Cometh in the Morning

Questions for Book Clubs and Discussion Groups

1. Did the book engage you immediately, or did it take you time to "get into it"?

2. What feelings/emotions did you experience as you were reading and what triggered them? Eg: amusement, anger, boredom, confusion, disgust, envy, fear, happiness, hope, love, pity, respect, sadness, etc.?

3. What were the main ideas the author sought to explore in her memoir?

4. Could you identify with any people? If so, which one(s) and why?

5. Which people were the strongest? The weakest?

6. Why do you think the people behaved as they did?

7. Do any people in the memoir remind you of people you know? If so, in what way(s)?

8. If you found yourself in the same situation as Patricia or others, do you think you would behave in the same way(s)?

9. Were you surprised by anything that happened to her or others?

10. Did any passages strike you as insightful, profound, or especially descriptive of human nature?

11. Why do you think the author chose to tell the story as she did?

12. Were you satisfied with the ending? If yes, why? If not, why not and how would you change it?

13. Did you learn anything from reading the story? If so, what?

14. If you met the author, what one question would you ask her?

Made in United States
North Haven, CT
01 May 2024

51996404R00114